SARAH BROWN'S NEW VEGETARIAN KITCHEN

BBC BOOKS

Food photography: Martin Brigdale
Home economist: Berit Vingrad
Stylist: Andrea Lambton
Illustrations: Lorraine Harrison

Published by BBC Books,
A division of BBC Enterprises Ltd,
Woodlands, 80 Wood Lane,
London W12 0TT

First published 1987

ISBN 0 563 20582 2 (paperback)
ISBN 0 563 20581 4 (hardback)

Typeset in 11/13pt Bembo by Phoenix Photosetting, Chatham
Printed and bound in Great Britain by Mackays of Chatham Limited
Colour printed by Chorley & Pickersgill

SARAH BROWN'S
→ NEW ←
VEGETARIAN
KITCHEN

To my father and mother

CONTENTS

INTRODUCTION

It has been a great pleasure writing this book, as I am happiest when experimenting in the kitchen creating new recipes and trying out different or unusual ingredients. From start to finish it is a voyage of discovery, and it is very rewarding to be able to pass on ideas, tips and suggestions that I hope will help you to cook more skilfully and improvise more confidently.

It is only three years on from my first book, *Vegetarian Kitchen*, and in that short time the changes both to our diet and our attitude to food have been tremendous. Vegetarians are certainly no longer the stereotype caricatured by wholemeal sandals and home-knitted yoghurt. The diet we eat is now widely recognised as being healthier, cheaper and just as delicious as any other. I hope you will discover this too when using these new recipes, and that you will find them easy to integrate into your way of life. Certainly the more commonplace vegetarian food becomes, the more benefit there will be to both human and animal kind.

As always, I owe a debt of gratitude to the many people who have helped me with this book, particularly Harriet Cruickshank who guided and encouraged me whenever I needed it; thanks also to Roselyne Masselin, Beverley Muir and Jo Wright for their generous help in creating and tasting recipes; Chris Glazebrook and Liz Storer for typing the original manuscript; Barbara Croxford for editing the recipes, Barry Hampshire for his invaluable help with the text, Ann Thompson for the design and Nina Shandloff for co-ordinating the project so patiently. I am also very grateful to Arthur Francis of Chennell and Armstrong, who gave me so much advice about wine, and to Chalie Amatyakul of the Oriental Cookery School, Bangkok, for introducing me to Thai cuisine. Many other friends have contributed in some way to this book by sharing an enthusiasm for food, eating up left overs, and putting up with a disrupted kitchen, so my thanks go to Pauline Ashley, Tim Buckland, Roger Chown, Stuart Craig, Michael Hunter, Greg MacLeod, Kaye Murdock, Ron Murdock and David Sulkin.

CREATING VEGETARIAN MEALS

I hope this book will help to familiarise you with the function and purpose of a wide range of vegetarian and wholefood ingredients, help you cook vegetarian food creatively and improvise with confidence.

The western world is undergoing a radical and dramatic shift in attitudes to good food and imaginative cooking, and for many reasons people are wanting to make a change in their diet, eating less meat and more wholefoods. There seems to be a growing recognition that the phrase 'You are what you eat' is absolutely true, coupled with an increasing awareness of how our health is affected by diet. You can hardly get round a supermarket these days without bumping into people looking up the latest E-number or food additive! The National Advisory Committee on Nutritional Education (NACNE) recommendations – eat less fat, sugar and salt, and eat more fibre – are slowly filtering through.

How much we want to change our diet will vary greatly from one person to another, and the changes certainly do not need to be wholesale or devastating. Everyone who cooks every day can get stuck in a rut, but changes can be made by simply taking on board one or two new techniques, introducing some different ingredients and building a new repertoire.

As you become more successful with vegetarian cookery, you will find it increasingly easy to be creative and to see how versatile the dishes can be. Several starters can be used to make a main course; different ideas go together very easily. Many hot dishes are equally good cold; sweet and savoury ingredients combine happily. Ideas for vegetarian cookery come from all over the world, so your culinary horizons will inevitably expand to cover a wide range of styles, flavourings and techniques. There are conventional meals to be made and served in the western style of 'meat and two veg', but it is just as easy to put together other meals composed of many different small dishes, or make an all-in-one pilaf or pilau. Why not mix and match dishes from very different cultures? Polenta, for example, is a classic Italian dish, but I think it is delicious served with a tasty Mexican spiced sauce.

It's fun to feel adventurous when cooking, but this is difficult unless you feel confident about the basic principles and ingredients to be used. Wholefoods and vegetarian ingredients can still seem very mysterious. It is often difficult to imagine how all the dehydrated items in the health food shop can become food or, when confronted with a pile of vegetables, to know how to give the meal a focus.

You can, of course, follow every recipe in this book to the letter, but I have tried in the introductions, where appropriate, to explain why certain ingredients are used and what their effect will be on the recipe so you can improvise more easily. I have used a much wider selection of ingredients than in my earlier book *Vegetarian Kitchen* but I have suggested alternatives, so if you don't have (or cannot get) one ingredient, you can replace it with something else.

Where possible at the beginning of a chapter or section, I have outlined a 'blueprint' recipe, either giving basic quantities or a full recipe. For instance, there is a basic vegetable soup, bean pâté, savoury flan, hotpot and a curry. Once you get an idea of the principles behind a recipe and the proportions of ingredients needed, you can easily experiment for yourself.

Apart from suggesting alternative ingredients in the recipes themselves, I have tried to show how you can make whole recipes more versatile by not limiting their use. For example, the pasta chapter contains a selection of sauces, so that you can choose the type of pasta you want to serve it with. Alternatively, I have suggested serving the pasta sauces with grains, gnocchi, polenta or vegetables. A salad dressing need not be limited to one mixture of vegetables, so a variety of ways in which the dressing would work well are also suggested.

Most of the classic pastry recipes are covered, except that they are converted to use wholewheat flour, and I have explained where best to use them. You will also find techniques for making different types of pancakes from Europe, India and Mexico, making flavoured stocks, cooking other whole grains besides rice, and using alternatives to dairy produce, such as tofu, nut milks and soya milks.

One frequent criticism of wholefood and vegetarian cookery is that it takes so much time and preparation. I think this can be true when you are unfamiliar with ingredients and trying new recipes. To help with this I have generally put the quicker and easier recipes towards the beginning of each chapter, with the more elaborate and time-consuming ideas at the end. Usually the quicker dishes are the ones that are useful for everyday meals, and those involving more preparation should be saved for special occasions.

CHANGING YOUR DIET

Anyone considering changing their diet should remember there is no right or wrong way to do it, and certainly no time limit. It has to fit in with how you feel, your lifestyle and the needs of your family. A new regime including more wholefoods and vegetarian meals can develop quite unconsciously – many people tell me how they have suddenly realised that they are eating less meat. Other people prefer to plan and deliberately give up one meat one month, and so on. You may feel like taking the plunge and dramatically altering everything overnight – which is fine as long as your family are supportive and willing – but a gradual approach is probably the easiest.

As a cook you must remember that you will need time to get used to different ingredients, and that shopping and preparation may take more time at first. It is best to go for familiar foods and familiar styles of meal in the early stages, gradually building up a repertoire of successful dishes that you can rely upon and make quickly. From there you can start to experiment. You will come across unexpected tastes and flavours, some of which will need to be acquired, but try not to be put off if you do not like some less familiar foods straight away.

COOKING FOR A 'MIXED' FAMILY

If your family is split about eating a wholefood or vegetarian diet – and I really admire cooks who prepare both meat and non-meat meals, especially if it goes against their basic principles – you will have to make full use of the freezer, microwave, and other electrical equipment that saves time when making larger quantities. At least then you can prepare extra portions to be frozen and kept for later. Don't forget, though, there are plenty of recipes that will satisfy everybody. It is very important to use wholefoods as the basis of these meals so that those who are vegetarians, or nearly so, get proper nutrients.

There are many meals that are meatless but not obviously so – dishes such as hearty casseroles, baked beans, quiches with eggs and vegetables, pies and pasta are acceptable and enjoyed by everyone. You may not be able to change attitudes but you can certainly change tastes.

COOKING FOR CHILDREN & ADOLESCENTS

Children are often difficult to please and as they are all different it is awkward to make hard and fast rules about how to encourage them to change to a healthy diet. I remember vehemently disliking Brussels sprouts at school and endeavouring to get rid of them at all costs, even if it meant the pocket of my tunic, only to be told that they were good for me. Ironically, they are now one of my favourite vegetables.

It is probably best if you can start children on a wholefood diet when they are babies. Of course, that is not always possible, and even children who have always been used to this type of diet may need more positive encouragement once they start school.

Remember that many of the most popular children's foods such as burgers, beans, pizzas and pasta can be good nutritious meals if they are made with wholefood ingredients. Introduce different herbs and spices gradually, so children can get used to more sophisticated flavours.

Take full advantage of the food processor. Vegetables and pulses that you think they may not like or will pick out, can be easily ground up and disguised in a sauce or soup – serve a nutritious soup with wholewheat bread for a good meal. Children may also like plain vegetables and it is easy to make these more nutritious with a cheese sauce or more colourful with a tomato sauce.

While wholefoods provide a sound nutritional basis, too much fibre in the diet can lead to small children becoming unable to absorb enough protein. You can overcome this problem by using concentrated forms of protein at main meals – tofu is ideal, especially as it has virtually no flavour and can be blended into many different dishes. Cheese and eggs should also be used.

One interesting statistic is that at present the largest concentration of vegetarians is among girls between the ages of 16 and 24. Certainly in many families of my acquaintance the move towards wholefoods has actually started with the adolescent members, but if this isn't the case with your teenagers you may have a rebellion on your hands when you want to change your diet. If you think they are going to want to pick at food rather than have main meals, try to provide plenty of fresh fruit, wholewheat bread and wholesome savouries, so at least the snacks can be nutritious. Have good quality cereals and plenty of nourishing spreads, such as nut butters and sugar-free jams, available. Remember that fast food – provided at home – isn't necessarily junk food, and the familiar baked potato should not be ignored as the basis of a good meal.

PLANNING MENUS

Vegetarian meals are extremely versatile. Often the same item of food can be used in sweet or savoury dishes and eaten at breakfast, lunch and supper. There are conventional style meals to be made, and ideas are also drawn from a great variety of cuisines. New and exotic foods are now more readily available, so new recipes can be invented to incorporate them. For these reasons, vegetarian meals provide enormous possibilities, but this can also be daunting if you are not sure where to begin. There are a few basic points to keep in mind.

↙ Try not to repeat a similar ingredient at each course – for example, a cashew nut soup followed by hazelnut roast and almond pudding. This may seem obvious but it can happen quite easily.

↙ Always make sure of a good mixture of flavours, textures and colours. Liquid dishes need a dry accompaniment, so serve a soup or casserole with a grain or pasta dish, potato or bread. Alternatively, make a crumble topping, pastry case or crunchy base to provide a contrast to a moist filling.

↙ Dry dishes such as burgers or bakes need a sauce or a moist accompaniment such as a vegetable purée. Rich mixtures containing nuts, cheese or high fat ingredients benefit from something fruity or slightly acidic. Floury textures of grains and pulses need enriching with a creamy ingredient or sharper taste like the delicate tang of yoghurt or counteracting with a citrus juice. Grains benefit particularly by being mixed with some lemon or orange juice, or a mild cider vinegar. The oriental flavourings of miso, shoyu, ginger and dry sherry work well with both floury and bland flavours. Where possible, marinate beans and grains when just cooked so they can absorb any dressing as they cool.

↙ If the main course you choose is predominantly vegetable, then select side dishes or starters that rely on other ingredients. A nut or cream soup could precede stuffed aubergines, a pilaf would go well with a vegetable curry, or a barley dish with a hotpot. Serve a bean dish such as butter bean salad with a vegetable pie or quiche. Side dishes such as these can often be made from ingredients kept in the store cupboard, so you don't have to worry about shopping. They also need little more preparation than soaking, if necessary, and cooking. Both these factors will save time.

The more you cook vegetarian foods, the quicker you will become at preparing them, as you start to use the foods without thinking and having to check on how they should be prepared and cooked. Ways of saving time will be obvious as you become familiar with the items that need the least preparation and meals which take very little time to cook. Buckwheat, millet and bulgar wheat are the quickest grains to cook, and there's no need to soak them overnight. Grain dishes usually need little preparation and there are many recipe ideas that can be cooked in one saucepan, keeping washing-up to a minimum. Lentils, split peas and small beans, such as aduki, cook quickly and, again, there is no soaking involved. These ingredients can be used as the basis for pies and pasty fillings, savoury crumbles or substantial spreads. I have mentioned many instances where dishes need sauces. If you are short of time, make vegetable purées instead, or use yoghurt, tofu or crème fraîche as the basis of a sauce. Nut butters and nut milks can also be used. A sauce used with plain pasta can act as the centrepiece of a quick meal. It is easy to make fast protein meals from tofu, cheese or eggs.

Don't forget to make the most of electrical equipment such as the food processor, or the freezer and microwave, so you can prepare in advance, freeze if necessary and reheat quickly. There is more information on equipment on pages 222–7.

When you are planning your first vegetarian menus, it may help to stick to tried and tested formulae. Have a central focus to the meal, such as a pie, pasty, burger or a bake, and a couple of contrasting accompaniments so that the meal looks as familiar as possible. Quiches make an excellent centrepiece for a cold meal. It is easier to recreate dishes you know well, giving them a vegetarian slant – pizzas, lasagne, vegetables in a cheese sauce, casseroles with mashed potato toppings.

As you become more confident, you can begin to think of using the foods in a different way, and the structure of the meal can change. There is no reason not to have several small complementary dishes making up the meal. This is prevalent in many eastern culinary cultures such as India. A thali may be served consisting of small portions of main and side dishes, often with a bread or rice accompaniment and a dessert on the same plate. In the Middle East, the mezze tradition is important. Here a large assortment of dishes are offered so each person can make their own choice. This is also a good way to entertain as everyone can have what they like best. An alternative way to structure a meal is to serve dishes separately rather in the French style, where the vegetables and meat are eaten as different courses. This can be done equally well with vegetarian dishes, and saves worrying about whether individual items or flavours go together.

To put together menus from this book, feel free to 'mix and match' all sorts of ideas. Bear in mind the points mentioned earlier, and avoid choosing too many dishes that need masses of preparation or last minute attention. Don't feel you have to stick to dishes from one country.

Below I have suggested several ideas for menus, some loosely based around an ethnic theme, others a little more conventional. There are also two suggestions for a collection of small dishes from which your guests can help themselves at a buffet-style meal. Consider all the following suggestions simply as a guide, adding extra courses or subtracting side dishes according to the numbers you are entertaining and the time you have available.

EVERYDAY ENTERTAINING

These three menus could be used for all sorts of occasions. The main courses feature familiar foods suitable for serving to non-vegetarians, or useful if you are fairly new to a vegetarian diet.

Stuffed Dates with Miniature Cashew Scones, or *Fragrant Bean Soup*
Globe artichoke with Herb Vinaigrette
Carrot and Courgette Bake
Creamed Celeriac
Wild Rice Pilaf
Sautéed mushrooms, or braised red cabbage
Mincemeat and Apple Flan, with yoghurt or cream

Fruit Kebabs
Savoury Oatcakes
Vegetables à la Cloche, or *Baked Pumpkin with Leeks and Cream*
Tagliatelle
Banana and Sunflower Cake

Spinach and Cheese Croquettes, or
Summer Vegetable Cocktail

Lasagne with Nut and Wine Sauce, or
Rich Mushroom Risotto

Mixed leafy green salad with Herb Vinaigrette,
or Fresh Herb Salad

Julienne of carrots and courgettes

Thai Fruit Salad, or stewed Hunza apricots

Kaye's Scotch Cookies

AROUND THE WORLD

These five menus are based loosely around ideas drawn from the cuisines of Mexico, Thailand, Italy, India and the Middle East.

Avocado and Apple Dip,
with red pepper and cucumber crudités

Mexican Beans, with Fruity Barley or
Polenta and Cheese and Chilli Sauce

Steamed Courgettes, or baby sweetcorn

Pineapple Sorbet

Spiced Cashew Nuts with Chilli

Tom Yam

Thai Fruit Salad

Red Kidney Bean Curry

Deep Fried Greens, or steamed mangetout

Spiced Millet

Yoghurt Ice Cream

Shades of Green Salad, or Butter Bean Salad

Pasta with Marinated Vegetable Sauce

Steamed French beans

Ricotta Cheesecake with strawberries

Tempura Vegetables with Yoghurt Dressing, or
Piquant Bean Pâté

Rice with Orange and Raisin Korma

Fragrant Vegetable Curry, or
Spiced Lentil and Vegetable Curry

Cumin Pancakes

Thai Coconut Custard, or fresh fruit

Fennel and Celeriac Soup, or Aubergine Dip

Persian Rice and Millet Ring, or
Bulgar Wheat Pilaf and Spiced Yoghurt

Tofu and Vegetable Stir-fry, or La Kama

Carrot salad

Special Muesli, or Banana and Carob Ice Cream

FORMAL DINNERS

These two menus feature main courses which look particularly impressive as centrepieces for more formal occasions.

Chestnut and Tomato Soup, and Seven Seed Bread

Layered Pancake Galette, and Honeyed Radishes

Potato Salad, or
cauliflower with Cottage Cheese Dressing or
Rich Paprika Mayonnaise

Carob Rum Trifle

Asparagus Soup with Almond Cream
Aduki Bean and Chestnut Loaf
Herb Roasted Vegetables, or baked parsnips
Steamed broccoli
Tomato sauce
Rhubarb and Banana Crumble

BUFFET MEALS

These two menus are for buffet lunches or help-yourself suppers, using slightly more unusual dishes than flans and salads. The second has a Middle Eastern theme. Both menus could make fork meals, or you could prepare just the finger food recipes for a party.

Chilled Tomato and Orange Soup
Sunflower Soufflés
Toasted Nut Burgers
Wheat with Celery and Sunflower Seeds
Choux pastry with Courgette and Cheese Dip, or Roquefort Eclairs
Brioche Buns
Stuffed Tomatoes
Carob and Orange Cake

Chick Pea and Spinach Pâté
Bulgar Wheat Croquettes
Sesame Bread Sticks
Red Pepper and Sunflower Dip
Tyropitas
Artichoke and Asparagus Salad, or Mangetout and Sesame Salad
Rice Bread with Sesame Seeds and Honey
Greek yoghurt
Fresh fruit: peaches, apricots and pomegranates

HERBS AND SPICES

Herbs and spices have always played a vital supporting role in cooking, each imparting its characteristic flavour to soups, stews, sauces and many other dishes. Cooks around the world have their ways of using them in many interesting combinations to add a special quality to a dish, to complement an ingredient, enhance a flavour, add nutrients or aid digestion. Vegetarian and wholefood cookery particularly benefits from a knowledgeable use of herbs and spices. Start by picking out classic mixtures from various cuisines and transposing them to your own recipe and, as you get more adventurous, you will be able to add different tastes to familiar meals, invent new dishes and give your cooking a personal style. The wider the range used, the more scope for experimenting.

Try to use fresh herbs: you can even grow your own. If you do use dried herbs, buy them from a busy shop, where the turnover is fast, and use them fairly quickly. You will need smaller quantities of a dried herb than a fresh one in a recipe – a third to a half in most cases. Keep dried herbs out of the light and in a cool place to retain the flavours longer.

Now readily available, whole spices are superior in flavour to the ground variety, though they do take a little more time to prepare. The traditional way is to pound them in a pestle and mortar but an electric grinder is quicker and easier. This must be cleaned very thoroughly after use; it is best to keep one exclusively for spices if possible. Ground spices should be stored in a cool dark place to preserve their flavour.

Many dishes benefit if simply flavoured with an individual herb, although there are some classic combinations such as bouquet garni, fines herbes and herbes de Provence. Spices are usually combined.

The only way to get a feel for any ingredient is to experiment with it. Be cautious when using herbs and spices at first. They are intended to enhance the flavour of the food, not overwhelm it. Below I have outlined the characteristics of thirty popular herbs and spices with their most frequent uses, plus some suggestions of how to combine them with other seasonings. This, of course, is just a starting point – the possibilities are almost endless.

Allspice

This spice can be bought whole or ground and is used in sweet dishes such as cakes and biscuits, as well as savoury recipes, particularly those from the West Indies and Middle East. Allspice complements barbecue flavours and tomato sauces, as well as providing an interesting aroma if used with grains.

Aniseed

Used in both sweet and savoury dishes, aniseed has a mild liquorice flavour. Popular in Mexican cookery, it provides a refreshing flavour and goes well with cheese, tomatoes and oriental flavours. Try aniseed with sweet nutty vegetables such as carrots, or red or white cabbage.

Basil

A mildly sweet, pungent herb primarily used in southern Mediterranean dishes. It is an essential ingredient in pesto (page 74). The flavour of basil goes particularly well with tomatoes, mushrooms, green beans, eggs and cheese. Use it for flavouring pizzas and pasta dishes, or chopping freshly into a salad. Dried basil is vastly inferior to the fresh leaves, in my opinion.

Bay Leaves

Bay has strongly flavoured leaves that need long cooking to release their aroma, so add them with the liquid when beginning to simmer a soup or stew. Their flavour goes well with barley, wheat, rice and root vegetables, and also imparts a nutty taste when infused with white sauces.

Caraway Seeds

Principally used in the cookery of northern Europe, these tangy seeds have a refreshing flavour. They have carminative properties which aid the digestion of rich or fatty ingredients such as cheese or nuts, and they counteract wind. Use caraway with green vegetables, in coleslaws and with the larger pulses such as red kidney or butter beans. Caraway works well when mixed with mustard seeds or thyme and paprika.

Cardamom

This seed has a strong perfumed flavour. It is used mainly in Middle Eastern and Indian cookery and is an ingredient in garam masala. The fragrant taste goes well with yoghurt and mild cheese, rice or millet dishes and curried vegetables.

Cayenne

Although a fiery hot spice, cayenne is milder than chilli; but be cautious when adding it to dishes. Use cayenne with Spanish-style dishes and to perk up lightly flavoured mixtures such as a batter or sauce, and provide a rich colour.

Celery Seeds

These tiny seeds have a pungent flavour, very reminiscent of celeriac. They can accentuate the taste of celery and go well with all root vegetable casseroles and delicately flavoured pasta and pancake sauces.

Chilli

The smaller and darker the chillies, the more powerful they are likely to be. The chilli seeds are more pungent and should be discarded. Used frequently in Mexican cookery, chillies combine well with earthy flavoured beans such as aduki beans or red kidney beans. In Indonesia they are mixed with garlic, ginger and coriander to flavour all sorts of dishes, especially those which include peanuts and coconut.

Chives

This herb has a delicate onion flavour which is lost if overcooked. Use snipped chives as last minute flavouring and for garnish. They complement creamy tofu or egg dishes, quiche fillings, salads, soya milk or dairy sauces, and the sweeter grains such as millet or barley.

Cinnamon

This spice is used in sweet dishes in western cuisine and for more savoury ideas in the East. Cinnamon is often used in Greek cookery mixed with oregano, and tastes delicious with aubergines and courgettes. Dried fruits flavoured with cinnamon make a delicious addition to grain dishes, particularly millet and rice.

Cloves

The pungent flavour of cloves can be used to counteract bready flavours so they make a good addition to a nut roast or pâté. Use them with an onion to infuse a white sauce or combine with stronger flavoured grains such as wheat and buckwheat.

Coriander

The seeds are spicy and aromatic and frequently combined with cumin, sometimes as part of a garam masala mixture. The fragrant taste blends well with the floury texture of pulses, particularly lentils and split peas. Combine coriander with dried fruits for sweet and savoury grain dishes. In Latin America it is frequently mixed with chilli and used in tomato and vegetable stews, cornmeal and polenta dishes. Fresh coriander is a wonderful herb. Use the leaves as a flavoured garnish, especially with grains. Chop the stems or root with garlic, lemon grass and chilli for full flavoured dishes.

Cumin

These seeds, with a pungent and penetrating flavour, work particularly well with coriander and are excellent with lentil dishes, such as soups, dhal or burgers. They can be used on their own with cabbage and carrot dishes. When lightly roasted, they are good with eggs, tofu or yoghurt.

Dill

This feathery herb has a mild aniseed flavour and makes a perfect flavouring garnish on salads or quiches. Dill complements floury textures and flavours, so combine it with potato, pastry and pancake dishes. Often dill is paired with paprika in the cookery of northern and eastern Europe.

Fennel

Rather like dill, but stronger in flavour, fennel seeds can be used with pulses to counteract their floury quality. Also add them to salads and barbecue sauces.

Garlic

One of the most widely used spices, garlic is either liked or hated. It is important to fry garlic properly at the start of a recipe and not to burn it as it will become bitter. Raw garlic used in salads and dips is invariably stronger and the effects more lasting.

Ginger

Try to buy the fresh root for use in savoury dishes. It has a delicious fresh, warm taste that works well with grain or pulse dishes. Ginger can be combined with either fiery or mellow spices. Use ground ginger for cakes, biscuits and puddings.

Mace and Nutmeg

These are linked together as the mace blades are the outer part of the nutmeg. Mace is more powerful and is excellent with cheese dishes, strongly flavoured vegetables such as spinach and grains such as buckwheat. Nutmeg is used in cream dishes and complements sweeter vegetables such as parsnips and carrots, and mild grains such as millet.

Marjoram and Oregano

These two herbs are closely related and have distinctive pungent flavours. They are frequently used in Spanish, Greek and Italian dishes, working well with pasta and tomato-based vegetable stews and sauces. Their flavours blend well with mushrooms and more watery vegetables such as marrow or aubergine. They are delicious in herb bread.

Mint

A wonderfully refreshing, well known herb which is excellent in salads as well as rice and pasta dishes.

Nutmeg See Mace.

Oregano See Marjoram.

Paprika

This versatile pepper has a mild sweet taste which adds a rich mellow flavour to pâtés, spreads, casseroles or grain dishes. Paprika is used frequently in Hungarian and Spanish cookery. It complements sour cream, mild cheese and tofu, as well as vegetables such as cauliflower, celery or potatoes. Use paprika with walnuts, pine kernels or almonds to enrich the base of a burger or bake.

Parsley

A delicious herb, full of vitamin C, which can be used freely in most savoury dishes, hot or cold. If you really enjoy the flavour of parsley, try the Fresh Herb Salad on page 187.

Rosemary

This herb has an aromatic flavour and also counteracts richness. Use rosemary with nuts and grains. Do make sure it is always well chopped as the needles of fresh rosemary can be quite sharp and dangerous.

Sage

A strongly flavoured herb that should be used sparingly. Always a difficult one to use for vegetarians as it is so reminiscent of sage and onion stuffing. However, sage does work well with bread-based dishes such as a nut burger or roast, also with the stronger grains like buckwheat. Add sage to cheese sauces too.

Tarragon

The subtle but distinctive flavour of tarragon blends well with light creamy dishes and can be used to flavour oils and vinegar for salad dressings. Use it with fresh pulses such as peas and broad beans, or in mashed dried pulses as the basis for a refreshing pâté or spread.

Thyme

This herb has a strong, penetrating flavour. Used in many English-style dishes, especially with vegetable casseroles, thyme is also frequently used with oregano in Spanish dishes of vegetables and rice. It is also good in pasta sauces and with vegetables such as potatoes or mushrooms.

Turmeric

Use turmeric, with its woody aroma, sparingly or the dish may become too pungent. Apart from the flavour, it adds a glorious yellow colour and is useful for making grain dishes and bean pâtés more appetising. I find a little turmeric added to green vegetables helps keep their colour bright.

SERVING WINE

There are no strict rules about which wine goes with which food, so often it is a matter of your own preference and budget. Here are some general guidelines to help you choose if you are not familiar with the flavours of vegetarian and wholefood dishes.

Full flavoured cream soups need a good tasty wine such as the Gewurztraminer based on the spicy grape from the Alsace. Richer soups, made with a nut base such as almonds or chestnuts, would be good with Montilla, a Spanish wine similar to sherry. A light vegetable soup should be accompanied with a tasty dry wine such as Mâcon Blanc. Accompany spiced soups with a Muscadet; look out for those described as Sur Lie which have a fuller flavour and are of a better quality. Another wine for serving with strongly flavoured soups is the Rioja Blanco Marques de Caceres. For chilled soups, such as the Summer Vegetable Cocktail (page 42), try any dry rosé such as Cavel. Other Vin de Table rosé wines tend to be dry so these would be a good alternative. Rosé d'Anjou has a touch of sweetness which could complement some chilled soups, or the sweeter vegetables served as crudités with a dip.

Fruit starters require wines with a refreshing bouquet such as a German Hock or Mosel. Alternatively choose from the English vineyards, such as Adgestone with its fragrant flavour, or Lamberhurst Priory.

Pâtés using vegetables or cheese as a base are often quite rich and are best served with a light red wine like Beaujolais Village, stronger in flavour than plain Beaujolais. Earthier flavoured pâtés, made with lentils or other pulses and some spicing, are good with a fuller red wine such as the Spanish Campo Viejo, a light Rioja. These wines have a distinctive flavour due to their long ageing in oak.

With pasta dishes, you may wish to serve red, rosé or white – so much will depend on the type of sauce and its consistency. A dry white such as Frascati would be good with a herb or creamy sauce, and light reds like Bardolino or Valpolicella are excellent with more fruity tomato flavours. Substantial pasta dishes such as lasagne or cannelloni with their earthy fillings need fuller flavoured wines like a Chianti. Look out for the Classico Reserva and the new Italian hallmark DOCG, which means the quality of the wine is guaranteed. Another good choice for this type of dish would be a New Zealand wine such as the Cooks Chardonnay.

For gnocchi, polenta or risotto dishes, where the base ingredient is floury in taste but the sauce may be rich, try a dry snappy wine such as Verdicchio or Gewurztraminer from the Trentino-Alto Adige (formerly the Tyrol). These wines also complement fondu style dishes.

For grain dishes with a Middle Eastern or Mediterranean touch, you will need a flavourful wine to match the spicing and in some cases the contrast of sweet and savoury ingredients. If you are lucky enough to come across the Lebanese Château Musar '79 vintage, it is to be recommended. Other good alternatives would be the Californian Chardonnay, Clos du Bois or the Bulgarian Merlot, which is a soft red wine.

More fully flavoured grain dishes, especially those with a hearty taste like buckwheat, and casseroles full of strong tasting vegetables such as peppers, aubergines and dried mushrooms, require big wines – generally red. A Cabernet Sauvignon from any country would be fine or go for the full flavoured Australian Shiraz wine.

Lighter main courses featuring a predominance of vegetables, cheese or cream sauces, served with pancakes or as a gratin, need robust white wines. A Bulgarian Pinot Chardonnay is quite dry and a little lean and would make a good choice especially as it is often a very reasonable price too. Savoury pastry dishes are also good with this wine, particularly flans and choux pastry. The Spanish Torres, a distinguished family firm, produce the flowery and fruity Gran Vino Sol which would go best with stuffed vegetables such as Baked Pumpkin (page 169) or Carrot and Courgette Bake (page 130).

Hot and spicy dishes such as curries really need beer!

Do look out for organic wines as an increasing number of independent growers now produce them. These wines are made from grapes which have not been sprayed with synthetic chemical pesticides, herbicides or fungicides. Producers of organic wines use plant based or herbal products to protect against crop damage and organic manure to enrich the soil. Organic red, white and rosé wines are available, particularly from France and some regions of Italy.

SOUPS & DUMPLINGS

T his is certainly a good chapter for starters! Soups are some of the easiest and most versatile dishes to make. Soup can be a sustaining meal on its own or if offered in traditional fashion at the beginning of a meal it can be warming in the winter months or light and refreshing served chilled in summer.

Here are some basic guidelines.

⚔ Use a good stock. I have given a useful all-round stock recipe, but if you are short of time, use a good quality vegetable concentrate or stock cube.

⚔ Don't forget there are other liquids apart from stock. Nut milks, cow's milk or soya milk will all add rich creamy flavours. Coconut and tofu can also be used to the same effect.

⚔ Sweat the vegetables to improve the overall flavour by cooking the onions over a gentle heat in a little oil, then adding the other vegetables.

⚔ Remember that making smooth soup need not be a chore. Thanks to the blender or food processor, soup that is going to be blended needn't be cooked for too long. But if you want a chunky version it will need longer so that the full flavour has a chance to develop. This type of recipe, too, may benefit from a small amount being puréed – about a third – then stirred back into the soup to improve the consistency. When blending soup, don't forget to allow the mixture to cool a little. Do not be concerned if the soup is thick at this stage, as any necessary liquid can be added later, when you can judge more easily whether the end result is going to be watery.

⚔ Decide before you start what the character of the soup is to be. Although the number of variations on vegetable soups seems limitless, don't just be tempted to throw together a whole batch of left overs or you will end up struggling to achieve a distinctive taste. Try to focus your idea around two or three ingredients and match those with a favourite herb or spice.

Soups can easily be accompanied by a choice of breads or savoury biscuits such as Sesame Bread Sticks (page 198) or Savoury Oatcakes (page 203); baked potatoes; a selection of raw vegetables (especially ones that contrast with the main ingredient of the soup); a platter of fresh fruit and cheese; or hot toasted sandwiches. Pasta or bulgar wheat will make the soup more robust. If you have a little more time, prepare the Dumplings on page 31.

A final word on preparation – most soups can be made well ahead of time so they can be chilled or reheated for serving. In general, soups freeze well.

BASIC VEGETABLE STOCK

Although there are many varieties of stock cubes available, it is easy and infinitely better to make your own stock. I find a pressure cooker especially useful for stock making as it is quick and seems to extract more flavour from the vegetables. Most root vegetables can be used for making stock – but remember that potatoes will make the liquid cloudy and do not use greens or brassicas as their flavour is too strong. Home-made vegetable stocks will be quite sweet. Counteract this by adding pungent herbs and spices such as bay leaf and celery seeds. I use a little oil to sweat the vegetables as it adds more flavour. The stock will keep several days in the refrigerator. Once you have a good basic stock, tasty soups are very quick to make. Do not necessarily throw away the flavouring vegetables, as they can be puréed and added to a thick soup. They do not really make a soup on their own, as their taste is too weak.

MAKES 1½ PINTS (900ML)
1 tablespoon sunflower oil
1 onion, peeled and cut into quarters
2 sticks of celery, trimmed and coarsely chopped
1 parsnip, peeled and cut into chunks
1 medium carrot, peeled and cut into chunks
2–3 parsley sprigs
1 bay leaf
½ teaspoon celery seeds
2 pints (1.1 litres) water

Heat the oil in a large pan or pressure cooker and cook the vegetables over a low heat for 5–6 minutes.

Add the parsley, bay leaf, celery seeds and water. Bring to the boil and simmer for 1–1½ hours or pressure cook for 20–25 minutes. Strain the stock and store in the refrigerator.

VEGETABLE SOUP

About 1–1½lb (450–700g) vegetables makes a good basis for a soup for 4 people. All sorts of combinations work well; in this recipe the sweetness of carrots and parsnips is balanced by the tomatoes and strongly flavoured cauliflower. Other good mixtures are leeks with mushroom and turnips, or with celery. If you do not have the time to make the vegetable stock, use the cooking liquid from pulses or vegetables. This can be stored in the refrigerator for several days, and you can mix different liquids when they are cool, provided the colour or flavour will not be too dominant. Alternatively, use some tomato purée, yeast extract, shoyu or miso, or a stock cube and extra herbs or spices.

MAKES 2 PINTS (1.1 LITRES)
1 tablespoon sunflower oil
1 onion, peeled and finely chopped
12oz (350g) mixed carrot and parsnip, peeled and diced
8oz (225g) cauliflower, divided into florets
1 × 14oz (400g) tin of tomatoes, mashed
¾ pint (450ml) vegetable stock
1 teaspoon prepared mustard
½ teaspoon creamed horseradish
1 teaspoon dried sage
salt and pepper

Heat the oil in a pan and gently cook the onion for 5 minutes or until soft. Add the carrot, parsnip and cauliflower and cook for 5 minutes, stirring frequently. Stir in the remaining ingredients. Bring to the boil, cover and simmer for 25–30 minutes.

Cool slightly, then purée half the vegetables with most of the liquid in a blender or food processor until very smooth. Return the soup to the pan. Season to taste and reheat for serving.

FRAGRANT BEAN SOUP

It is very useful to have cooked beans (see Pulses on page 232) on hand, either in the refrigerator or freezer, to turn a light meal into something more substantial. This soup is suitable for any type of brown or red bean. Beans provide protein, texture and a good earthy flavour that works well with spices, especially the warm fragrant mixture of coriander and paprika. Green vegetables complement the colour, but do not chop them too finely or the texture will be lost. Mash the cooked beans to enrich and thicken the cooking liquid.

MAKES 2 PINTS (1.1 LITRES)
1 tablespoon olive oil
1 onion, peeled and finely chopped
8oz (225g) courgettes, trimmed and diced
1 green pepper, deseeded and diced
8oz (225g) cooked brown beans, eg pinto or Dutch beans, mashed
1 teaspoon ground coriander seeds
1 tablespoon paprika
2 cloves garlic, crushed
1 teaspoon olive oil
1 pint (570ml) vegetable stock
salt and pepper
2–3 tablespoons chopped fresh coriander leaves

Heat the tablespoon of oil in a pan and gently cook the onion for 5 minutes or until soft. Add the courgettes and pepper, stir well and cook for 3–4 minutes. Stir in the mashed beans and cook for 2 minutes.

Mash the spices and garlic into the teaspoon of olive oil, using a pestle and mortar. Mix into the stock and pour over the vegetables, stirring well. Bring to the boil, cover and simmer for 25–30 minutes. Season to taste. Just before serving, add the fresh coriander.

LENTIL SOUP

Using lentils is an easy way to make a few different vegetables go much further and at the same time produce a tasty, nutritious soup. Red lentils are the most readily available of the pulses. They cook extremely quickly, breaking down to a thick golden cream. Other quick-cooking pulses are split green or yellow peas, or whole brown or green lentils. For a basic soup, use about 4–6oz (110–175g) dry weight of pulses plus 1¼–1½ pints (700–900ml) stock for 4 people. I find a sharp-tasting ingredient, such as citrus juice or a mild vinegar, counteracts the bland nature of the beans and lifts the overall flavour. Extra oil added at the beginning or end will enrich the soup. These quick-cooking pulses blend well with most vegetables. Either make relatively homely fare with various root vegetables, or try a ratatouille base with Mediterranean herbs or an Indian or Middle Eastern selection of spices and vegetables. Instead of the vegetable stock, use wine, tomato juice or coconut milk as they make an interesting difference to the soup.

MAKES 1¾ PINTS (1 LITRE)
1 tablespoon sunflower oil
2 medium leeks, cleaned and diced
2 sticks of celery, trimmed and diced
6oz (175g) turnip or swede, peeled and diced
6oz (175g) red lentils
1¼ pints (700ml) vegetable stock
1 bay leaf
2 teaspoons miso
2 tablespoons finely chopped fresh parsley
juice of ½ lemon
salt and pepper

Heat the oil in a large pan and gently cook the leeks for 3–4 minutes. Add the celery and turnip and cook for 5 minutes.

Pick over the lentils for stones, then rinse thoroughly and drain well. Add to the vegetables, mix in well and cook for 2–3 minutes. Pour over the stock and add the bay leaf. Bring to the boil, cover and simmer for 40 minutes, or cook for about 12 minutes in a pressure cooker.

Remove 2 tablespoons of liquid and dissolve the miso in it. Add to the pan with the parsley. Remove the bay leaf, then purée the soup in a blender or food processor until smooth and creamy. Add the lemon juice and adjust the seasoning. Reheat before serving.

CLEAR SOUP WITH NOODLES

It is most important to have a well flavoured stock for a clear soup. If you cannot obtain dried mushrooms, use 8oz (225g) fresh mushrooms.

MAKES 2 PINTS (1.1 LITRES)
8 dried Chinese mushrooms
2 pints (1.1 litres) hot, dark stock or bean liquid
1 clove garlic
1 teaspoon peppercorns
2 tablespoons chopped coriander root or lower stems
8oz (225g) firm tofu, diced
3 spring onions, chopped into 1 inch (2.5cm) lengths
2oz (50g) bamboo shoots
2oz (50g) wholewheat or buckwheat noodles
1–2 tablespoons shoyu

Soak the Chinese mushrooms in the hot stock for 2–3 hours. Drain the mushrooms, reserving the stock, and slice finely. Pound the garlic, peppercorns and coriander root together in a pestle and mortar.

Put all the ingredients, except the shoyu, into a pan. Bring to the boil and simmer for 25 minutes. Add the shoyu to taste just before serving.

DUMPLINGS

These enriched dumplings are ideal for turning a soup into a main meal.

MAKES 8
1½oz (40g) self-raising wholewheat flour
1½oz (40g) cornmeal
¾oz (20g) sunflower margarine
2 teaspoons herbes de Provence
pinch of chilli powder
1 small (size 6) egg
2 teaspoons natural yoghurt

Mix the flour, cornmeal and a pinch of salt in a bowl. Rub in the margarine until the mixture resembles fine breadcrumbs. Add the herbs and chilli powder. Beat the egg and yoghurt together. Add enough to the flour mixture to make a soft dough. Form into walnut-sized pieces.

Drop the dumplings into boiling liquid and cook for 7–8 minutes.

ASPARAGUS SOUP WITH ALMOND CREAM

Photograph opposite

Nut milks provide a very rich soup base, but one disadvantage is that they can over-thicken the liquid, making the soup rather heavy. Solve this problem by straining the almond milk through a fine sieve. The remaining pulp can be dried out in the oven or microwave and added to crumble mixtures or cereals as it still has some flavour. The mild taste of almond milk complements the delicate asparagus. Cashews could be used instead, but nut milks made from hazelnuts or walnuts are rather overpowering and are better used in savoury roasts.

MAKES 2 PINTS (1.1 LITRES)
6oz (175g) blanched almonds
2 pints (1.1 litres) light stock or water
1 tablespoon sunflower oil
4 sticks celery, trimmed and diced
1lb (450g) asparagus, trimmed and chopped, reserving a few tips for garnish
3 teaspoons fines herbes
2 tablespoons finely chopped fresh parsley
3–4 teaspoons tarragon vinegar
salt and pepper

Grind the almonds very finely in a blender or food processor. Add the stock and blend again until quite smooth. Sieve the liquid to remove any grains of almonds.

Heat the oil in a pan and gently fry the celery for 5–6 minutes. Add the asparagus and cook for 5 minutes. Pour over the almond milk and add the fines herbes and parsley. Simmer for 15 minutes.

Cool slightly, then purée in a blender or food processor until smooth. Add the tarragon vinegar and season to taste. Serve hot or chilled, garnished with the remaining asparagus tips.

Opposite: Asparagus Soup with Almond Cream (this page) and Miniature Cashew Scones (page 204)

CREAMED SWEET POTATO SOUP

Root vegetables, available for most of the year, make wonderful creamy soups without the need to add milk or cream, so the overall fat content is low. In this recipe, the floury character of sweet potato is counterbalanced with the sweetness of allspice and enriched with tomatoes. When experimenting with other root vegetables such as parsnips, swede, kohlrabi or carrots, try other spices such as nutmeg, mace, cinnamon or cardamom, or sharpen the flavour with orange, lemon or lime.

MAKES 2 PINTS (1.1 LITRES)
1 tablespoon peanut or groundnut oil
2 onions, peeled and finely chopped
1 green pepper, deseeded and diced
1lb (450g) sweet potato, peeled and diced
½ teaspoon ground allspice
1 teaspoon dried oregano
2 tablespoons finely chopped fresh parsley
1 × 7oz (200g) tin of tomatoes, mashed
1 pint (570ml) vegetable stock
salt and pepper
Garnish
chopped fresh parsley

Heat the oil in a pan and gently sweat the onion for 5–7 minutes or until soft, but not browned. Add the green pepper, sweet potato and allspice and stir in well. Cover and cook for 10 minutes, stirring occasionally. Add the oregano, parsley, tomatoes and stock. Bring to the boil and simmer for 15 minutes or until the sweet potato is well cooked.

Cool slightly, then purée in a blender or food processor until smooth. Season to taste. Reheat and garnish with parsley.

Opposite: Leek and Mushroom Ramekins (page 54); Red Pepper and Sunflower Dip (page 50); and Sesame Bread Sticks (page 198)

CHESTNUT AND TOMATO SOUP

Chestnuts are unlike other nuts as they are low in fat but high in starch, which means they can be used like a flour when thickening a liquid. They also have a fairly sweet flavour, which is counteracted in this recipe by tomatoes and aromatic caraway seeds. I do not think there is really any difference in the end result between using fresh or dried chestnuts, and the dried ones are convenient to keep in your store cupboard. Chestnut purée can be mixed with carob, chocolate or fruits for puddings, or used with other nuts for savoury roasts or loaves. To reconstitute dried chestnuts, soak first and cook in their soaking liquid. The resulting stock is very tasty and quite sweet; it can be used for a variety of sauces.

MAKES 1¾ PINTS (1 LITRE)
10oz (275g) fresh or 5oz (150g) dried chestnuts
1 tablespoon sunflower oil
2 leeks, cleaned and diced
1 clove garlic, crushed
1 teaspoon caraway seeds
1 × 14oz (400g) tin of tomatoes, mashed
⅔ pint (400ml) chestnut or Garlic Stock (page 37)
salt and pepper

Preheat the oven to Gas Mark 4, 350°F (180°C). Roast the fresh chestnuts for 15–20 minutes. Peel and chop the nuts. If using dried chestnuts, soak for 1 hour in boiling water. Bring the nuts to the boil in their soaking water and simmer for 35–40 minutes. Drain, reserving the stock.

Meanwhile, heat the oil in a pan and gently cook the leeks and garlic for 5–6 minutes, stirring once or twice. Add the prepared chestnuts and caraway seeds and cook for 2 minutes. Stir in the tomatoes and stock. Bring to the boil, cover and simmer for 30 minutes.

Cool slightly, then purée in a blender or food processor. For an extra smooth texture, sieve the soup. Season to taste and reheat before serving.

GARLIC STOCK

Although making a stock with so much garlic sounds daunting or unsociable, the liquid produced is rather creamy in appearance and fairly mild. This is an ideal stock to make when the final recipe needs to have a subtle underlying flavour with a rather elusive quality.

MAKES 1½ PINTS (900ML)
2 pints (1.1 litres) water
10 whole peeled cloves garlic
1 onion, peeled and halved
2 medium carrots, peeled and roughly chopped
1 turnip, peeled and roughly chopped
handful celery leaves

Put all the ingredients in a large pan. Bring to the boil and simmer for 1 hour. Alternatively, pressure cook for 20 minutes. Strain before using.

FENNEL AND CELERIAC SOUP

Celeriac, a member of the celery family, and fennel are very compatible vegetables. For success with this recipe, use Garlic Stock (above) as it makes the final purée extremely creamy and surprisingly rich, enhancing the fennel's anise flavour.

MAKES 1½ PINTS (900ML)
1 tablespoon sunflower oil
8oz (225g) fennel, diced
8oz (225g) celeriac, peeled and cut in julienne strips
1 tablespoon wholewheat flour
1 pint (570ml) Garlic Stock (page 37)
2–3 tablespoons Frascati white wine
salt and pepper

Heat the oil in a pan and gently sweat the fennel and celeriac, covered, for 10–15 minutes or until soft. Sprinkle over the flour and cook for 2–3 minutes, stirring. Add the stock and stir well. Bring to the boil, cover and simmer for 7 minutes.

Cool slightly, then purée half the ingredients in a blender or food processor to a smooth cream. Return to the pan. Add the wine and season to taste. Reheat before serving.

CREAMY MUSHROOM SOUP WITH TOFU

Tofu is such an important food it is worth getting to know and like it, even though initially its lack of flavour and texture may be off-putting. Remember tofu is like blotting paper: it soaks up any flavour. Once blended, it also helps to create a creamy base for soups as well as dips and sauces, without adding nearly so many calories or saturated fats as would milk or cream. Tofu also won't overpower the basic flavour. This mushroom soup is an ideal starter as the end result is light yet seemingly rich and creamy.

MAKES 1½ PINTS (900ML)
1 tablespoon sunflower oil
2oz (50g) shallots, peeled and chopped
12oz (350g) field mushrooms, wiped and quartered
1 teaspoon dried thyme
½ teaspoon grated nutmeg
⅔ pint (400ml) Garlic Stock (page 37)
4oz (110g) firm or silken tofu
1–2 tablespoons shoyu
salt and pepper

Heat the oil in a pan and fry the shallots for 5 minutes. Add the mushrooms, thyme and nutmeg, stir well, then cover and cook over a gentle heat for 5 minutes. Add the stock, bring to the boil and simmer for another 5 minutes.

Cool slightly, then purée with the tofu in a blender or food processor until completely smooth. Finally, add the shoyu and season to taste. Reheat gently before serving.

THAI SPICED SOUPS

TOM YAM

This is a spiced soup from Thailand, where the stock is made by pounding various herbs and spices together to make a smooth paste. The principal ingredients are normally coriander, peppercorns and chilli in varying proportions. Lemon grass and ginger are also widely used. Although it takes a little time, it is worth making the paste by hand in a pestle and mortar so that the oils are released more gradually and gently. Traditionally fish paste is used for a salty flavour, but I find miso is an ideal substitute. This soup could be made with other vegetables; mushrooms work particularly well.

MAKES 2 PINTS (1.1 LITRES)
2 tablespoons chopped coriander root or lower stems
3–4 teaspoons peppercorns
1 green chilli, deseeded
1 teaspoon grated fresh root ginger
3 stalks lemon grass
1½ pints (900ml) dark or Garlic Stock (page 37)
3 tablespoons lime juice
10oz (275g) carrots, peeled and diced
10oz (275g) sweetcorn, frozen or fresh
2 tablespoons roughly chopped fresh coriander leaves
1 teaspoon miso, dissolved in a little stock
salt

Pound the coriander root, peppercorns, chilli, ginger and lemon grass together in a pestle and mortar to a fairly smooth paste.

Put the paste, stock and lime juice into a large pan and simmer for 8 minutes. Add the carrot and sweetcorn and simmer for 30 minutes or until the carrots are tender. Stir in the coriander and miso just before serving. Season to taste if necessary.

CAULIFLOWER SOUP WITH GINGER

Coconut milk, widely used in Indonesian cookery, makes an excellent creamy stock and substitute for dairy products. Remember, though, that it is one of the few sources of saturated fats from the vegetable kingdom, so it should be eaten sparingly. Coconut milk is made by dissolving grated coconut cream in boiling liquid. The more liquid you use, the thinner the milk will be. For a very smooth consistency, strain the milk before using. This spicy soup is flavoured with ginger, garlic, chilli and coriander roots or stems, finely pounded to a smooth paste.

MAKES 2¼ PINTS (1.3 LITRES)

2 inch (5cm) piece fresh root ginger, grated
2 cloves garlic
½ teaspoon ground pepper
3 tablespoons chopped coriander root or lower stems
2 spring onions, trimmed and finely chopped
1 small chilli, deseeded and finely chopped
3½oz (90g) creamed coconut, grated
1 small cauliflower, about 12oz (350g), divided into florets
4oz (110g) mooli, peeled and diced
¾ pint (400ml) light stock
1–2 tablespoons lemon juice
salt

Pound the ginger, garlic, pepper, coriander, spring onion and chilli to a fine paste in a pestle and mortar.

Dissolve the creamed coconut in 1 pint (570ml) boiling water. Blend the liquid until smooth in a blender or food processor. Heat 2–3 tablespoons of the coconut milk and lightly braise the cauliflower and mooli, stirring well and adding a little more coconut milk if necessary. Add the stock and simmer for 10 minutes or until the cauliflower is tender.

Mix the spice paste into the remaining coconut milk and stir well. Add the spiced milk, and a little more stock if necessary, to the cauliflower and heat to boiling point, stirring frequently. Season with lemon juice and salt. Serve immediately.

CHILLED SOUPS

CHILLED TOMATO AND ORANGE SOUP

Although seemingly sweet, tomatoes are actually quite acidic. An old catering trick is to use some sugar in the stock, but I think it is preferable to add a sweet vegetable, such as carrot, and a little fruit juice. Yoghurt and wine vinegar add a tang which gives a more definite flavour, essential for a cold soup. If the day you have chosen for serving this soup turns out to be a typical cold summer day, serve it hot, but wait until just before serving to add the yoghurt in swirls, or it may curdle.

MAKES 1¾ PINTS (1 LITRE)
1 tablespoon sunflower oil
3oz (75g) shallots, peeled and chopped
2 medium carrots, peeled and diced
1 clove garlic
1 × 14oz (400g) tin of tomatoes, mashed
1 tablespoon paprika
juice of 2 oranges
2 teaspoons grated orange rind
½ pint (275ml) natural yoghurt
1–2 teaspoons white wine vinegar
salt and pepper

Heat the oil in a pan and fry the shallots over a gentle heat for 5 minutes. Add the carrots and garlic and cook for 5 minutes. Stir in the tomatoes and paprika, cover and cook for 20 minutes.

Cool slightly, then add the orange juice and rind. Purée in a blender or food processor until smooth. Stir in the yoghurt and vinegar and season to taste. Serve chilled.

SUMMER VEGETABLE COCKTAIL

A juicer is the sort of gadget that may well gather dust until you discover the marvellous flavours of freshly made vegetable juices, either plain or mixed to create cocktails. It is great fun experimenting. But as with all kitchen gadgets, they need to be easily accessible otherwise it just seems an extra chore to get them into use. You will certainly get the best results with this recipe if you use a juicer. A good alternative is to buy about ¾–1 pint (450–570ml) carrot juice, then purée the lettuce and watercress with the peas. Breadcrumbs thicken the juice for a more soup-like quality.

MAKES 1½ PINTS (900ML)
3lb (1.4kg) carrots, scrubbed
1 large lettuce
1 bunch of watercress
1 tablespoon concentrated apple juice
2 tablespoons lemon juice
1–2 tablespoons sunflower oil
4oz (110g) fresh wholewheat breadcrumbs
1lb (450g) peas
1 tablespoon finely chopped fresh mint
Garnish
1 red-skinned apple, very thinly sliced

Blend the carrots, lettuce and watercress in a juicer (see above). Mix the juice with the concentrated apple juice, lemon juice, oil, breadcrumbs, peas and mint. Purée in a blender or food processor until smooth. Strain through a fine sieve. Serve chilled, garnished with slices of apple.

PÂTÉS, DIPS & SPREADS

Recipes for pâtés and spreads need to be in the repertoire of any cook – vegetarian or otherwise. They can be light meals in themselves or a good starting point for packed lunches. Pâtés also add interest to a buffet or picnic spread.

It is hard to know where a pâté ends and a spread begins! Pâté and terrine were words used to describe traditional meat-based dishes baked in the oven in an earthenware dish or a pastry case. In vegetarian terms, a pâté, dip or spread can be made from beans, nuts or vegetables – either cooked and puréed, finely ground or diced and set into a thick sauce. What it is called depends on the consistency. The simplest versions are made with a plain purée flavoured with herbs and spices and enriched with nut butters, oils or mayonnaise. The possibilities are endless and I have given some guidelines with the bean pâté recipes so that you can see how to experiment.

Pulses are good to use because they are nutritious and cheap and will marry up with a large range of flavours. Vegetables, nuts and seeds also work well, and recipes using these are included, such as the Courgette and Cheese Dip or Red Pepper and Sunflower Dip.

All these simple pâtés and dips can be served on their own. Alternatively, choose two or three contrasting ones, pile them into attractive serving dishes and group with pickles, cheese and salads for a splendid party spread. Make individual servings with scoops of different coloured mixtures and accompany with crudités – attractively cut pieces of raw vegetables. Do not chop vegetables for crudités until shortly before serving and, once prepared, keep them cling-film wrapped and chilled. Make sure there are plenty as they are 'more-ish' and present them in an attractive way – either grouped together in a napkin-lined basket or arranged in contrasting colour groups on a large plate. You can concentrate on a one- or two-colour theme, such as shades of green – courgettes, beans, celery and chicory – or red and white – mushrooms, cauliflower florets, red pepper and carrot. Do not just think of crudités for the summer, as there are plenty of vegetables that can be eaten raw during the winter months too. Avoid vegetables or fruits that discolour easily such as avocados, celeriac or apples. If you are just getting used to the idea of eating vegetables raw, you can mix in some that are lightly blanched, such as cauliflower, Brussels sprouts and broccoli.

Pâtés can be presented in scooped-out vegetables. Tomatoes, small peppers, celery sticks or leaves of chicory are all suitable containers. Alternatively, wrap pâtés in lettuce or vine leaves, or young spinach leaves, turning them into more interesting party snack food. Firmer pâtés can be shaped into pieces and rolled in chopped nuts or herbs.

The simplest spreads of all for sandwiches or canapés are nut butters, such as peanut butter. This is readily available from wholefood shops and supermarkets – though do buy a sugar-free variety. Look for almond, hazel and cashew nut butters or make your own by grinding your choice of nut finely and adding a little oil.

Most of the pâtés and dips in this chapter could be used for sandwich and pitta bread fillings. This certainly solves one problem of getting variety in packed lunches. Use beansprouts, particularly alfalfa, or salad cress to give extra moisture and a crisp texture. Don't forget that a pâté will last several days in the refrigerator so you can make a sizeable batch.

Apart from giving a blueprint idea for experimenting with bean purées to create basic pâtés, I have included simple recipes using other staple ingredients such as vegetables, nuts and seeds.

At the end of the chapter there are two elaborate baked pâté recipes that will take a little more time to prepare but are well worth the effort.

BEAN PÂTÉS

All of the pulse family – beans, peas and lentils – can be used to make tasty and interesting pâtés, spreads and dips. I think they are ideal as a base because they provide colour and texture, are quite substantial and blend easily with a whole variety of different flavourings.

Soft pâtés or spreads can be made from a cooked bean purée with other ingredients added later. If you need a more robust dish, one that will stand up to being cut in slices, add an egg or a binding agent such as tahini. Adding breadcrumbs will give the pâté a firmer texture but also a bready quality, so be sure to flavour the basic mixture well. Bake this type of pâté in the oven. Alternatives to breadcrumbs are flakes and meals. Porridge oats are particularly useful as they are rich and creamy but do not make the end result too heavy.

Apart from using herbs and spices, you can make bean purées more flavoursome with chutneys, fruit juices and citrus rinds, wines and vinegars. Oils, nut butters, cream, cottage cheese and mayonnaise will all enrich these pâtés. Vegetables, raw or cooked, finely chopped or puréed, add colour, change the texture and make the end result more moist.

I have suggested five sets of ingredients for flavouring a plain bean purée. Use red kidney beans or broad beans and peas for earthy coloured pâtés, and white or pale yellow beans for creamy versions. All bean pâtés are best made in advance to allow the flavours to develop. Serve with bread or biscuits or as part of a cold buffet or as a starter.

PIQUANT BEAN PÂTÉ

This bean purée is enhanced by a herb and mustard vinaigrette.

SERVES 4–6
6oz (175g) red kidney or dark beans, soaked overnight
2 tablespoons olive oil
2 tablespoons red wine
1 teaspoon prepared French mustard
1 teaspoon chopped fresh tarragon
1 clove garlic, crushed

Drain the beans and rinse well. Place in a pan and cover with plenty of fresh water. Bring to the boil and boil fiercely for 10 minutes, then simmer for 40 minutes or until soft. Drain well and purée. Mash in the remaining ingredients and leave to cool.

COUNTRY BEAN PÂTÉ

Breadcrumbs give this pâté a more defined texture.

SERVES 4–6
6oz (175g) red kidney or dark beans, soaked overnight
2 tablespoons tomato purée
2 tablespoons shoyu
1 tablespoon chopped fresh parsley
2oz (50g) fresh wholewheat breadcrumbs
1 teaspoon lemon juice
1 teaspoon paprika
1 clove garlic, crushed

Drain, cook and purée the beans as above. Mash in remaining ingredients and leave to cool.

CREAMED BEAN PÂTÉ

The floury quality of the beans can be enriched with mayonnaise and sharpened with fresh herbs and a hint of citrus.

SERVES 4–6
6oz (175g) butter or pale beans, soaked overnight
2 tablespoons mayonnaise
1 tablespoon lemon juice
2–3 tablespoons finely chopped fresh mint, chives or parsley
salt and pepper

Drain, cook and purée the beans as on page 46. Mash in the remaining ingredients and leave to cool.

SPICED BEAN PÂTÉ

The flavour of this pâté is enhanced by toasted cumin and sesame seeds.

SERVES 4–6
4oz (110g) Dutch brown or pinto beans, soaked overnight
1 tablespoon sesame seeds
1 teaspoon cumin seeds
4 spring onions, trimmed and very finely chopped
1–2 cloves garlic, crushed
3 tablespoons tahini
1 tablespoon tomato purée
1/2oz (15g) fresh parsley, finely chopped
1 tablespoon lemon juice
salt and pepper

Drain the beans and rinse well. Place in a pan and cover with fresh water. Bring to the boil and boil fiercely for 10 minutes, then cover and simmer for 25–30 minutes or until soft. Drain and mash well.

Toast the sesame and cumin seeds together in a dry frying pan or under the grill for 3–4 minutes. Grind finely in a pestle and mortar. Mix the beans, seeds and remaining ingredients together, stirring thoroughly.

Leave the pâté to stand for several hours or overnight. Adjust the seasoning to taste before serving.

BEAN AND ALMOND PÂTÉ

Nuts enrich a bean purée, adding fat to the mixture. You could use a nut butter instead of ready-ground nuts for a richer version.

SERVES 4–6
6oz (175g) butter or pale beans, soaked overnight
2oz (50g) ground almonds
1 tablespoon natural yoghurt
2 teaspoons sunflower oil
1 tablespoon finely chopped fresh parsley
salt and pepper

Drain, cook and purée the beans as on page 46. Mash in the remaining ingredients and leave to cool.

CHICK PEA AND SPINACH PÂTÉ

When using spinach in a vegetable pâté, drain it thoroughly both before and after cooking or the end result can be watery. I find a small amount of turmeric added to a green purée highlights the colour. This pâté could also be used as a filling for a pasty or filo pastry.

SERVES 4–6
4oz (110g) chick peas, soaked overnight
1 teaspoon turmeric
1 onion, peeled and quartered
1lb (450g) spinach, washed
1 clove garlic, crushed
2 tablespoons finely chopped fresh coriander
2 teaspoons finely chopped fresh mint
1/2 teaspoon ground cumin
2 tablespoons olive oil
2 tablespoons lemon juice
1/2 teaspoon grated lemon rind
salt and pepper

Drain the chick peas. Place in a pan, cover with fresh water and add the turmeric and onion. Bring to the boil and boil fiercely for 10 minutes, then cover and simmer for 25–30 minutes. Drain and finely grind in a blender or food processor.

Roughly chop the spinach. Wilt for 2–3 minutes in a covered pan over a moderate heat. Purée in a blender or food processor. Combine the chick peas and spinach with the remaining ingredients and mix thoroughly.

Leave the pâté to stand for several hours or overnight. Adjust the seasoning to taste before serving.

VEGETABLE DIPS

COURGETTE AND CHEESE DIP

When using vegetable pureés for dips, the texture needs strengthening, and in this recipe a soft cheese has been added. It is also essential to keep the initial purée as dry as possible, so squeeze out all the moisture from the courgettes using a wooden spoon and strong sieve.

SERVES 4
8oz (225g) courgettes, trimmed
½ teaspoon salt
1oz (25g) fresh continental or flat parsley, finely chopped
1oz (25g) sunflower margarine or butter
3oz (75g) curd cheese or quark
pepper

Grate the courgettes very finely. Sprinkle with the salt and leave for 30 minutes.

Squeeze out any excess moisture from the courgettes. Purée with the parsley in a blender or food processor until just blended. Do not over-blend or the resulting pâté will be too liquid.

Cream the margarine with the curd cheese, then beat in the courgette mixture until smooth. Season and chill for 1–2 hours or until firm.

AVOCADO AND APPLE DIP

Rich, buttery avocado is ideal as a basis for a smooth dip. Guacamole is a traditional Mexican recipe, in which the avocado flesh is mixed with garlic, lemon juice and oil (see page 109). I like to counteract the richness of the avocado with tiny pieces of apple and red pepper; these are both moist and refreshing, and break up the smooth texture. Use this dip with raw vegetables or as a filling for sandwiches or pitta bread.

SERVES 4

1 dessert apple, preferably red-skinned
juice of ½ lemon
1 ripe avocado, peeled and stoned
2 tablespoons mayonnaise
½ red pepper, deseeded and finely chopped
salt and pepper
Optional Extras
1 tablespoon pine kernels
1 tablespoon sunflower seeds

Core and very finely dice the apple. Toss in the lemon juice and leave for 10–15 minutes.

Mash the avocado flesh and mix with mayonnaise. Add the apple, lemon juice and red pepper. Stir well, then season to taste.

For a crunchier version, lightly toast the nuts and seeds under the grill for 3–4 minutes. Cool and stir into the avocado mixture.

RED PEPPER AND SUNFLOWER DIP

Photograph on page 34

The vibrant colours of red and yellow peppers make them a joy to use. I am sure also that anyone who finds peppers indigestible should try this recipe, as they may find them acceptable once they are skinned and puréed. The delicate nutty flavour of the sunflower seeds blends in very well, without overpowering the taste of the peppers. A hint of orange enhances the sweetness. I have also used this dip, thinned down with fruit juice or water, as a sauce for Lentil and Walnut Burgers (page 65).

SERVES 4
2 large red peppers
4oz (110g) sunflower seeds
2 tablespoons cider vinegar
1 teaspoon grated orange rind
1 tablespoon sunflower oil
½ teaspoon ground allspice
salt and pepper

Preheat the oven to Gas Mark 4, 350°F (180°C). Bake the peppers for 25–30 minutes or until the outer skin is well charred. Peel off the outer skin and remove any seeds or pith. Chop the flesh.

Meanwhile, toast the sunflower seeds in the oven for 5–10 minutes until lightly browned. Grind very finely in a nut mill or coffee grinder. Add the peppers and remaining ingredients to the sunflower seed powder and mix thoroughly. Leave to stand, overnight if possible. Adjust the seasoning before serving with crudités, bread sticks or oatcakes.

AUBERGINE DIP

There are many versions of aubergine pâtés and dips in Middle Eastern cuisines. I add tofu to give the dip a creamy look and texture, and to lighten the flavour. The tamarind provides a wonderful, slightly sour taste. Once the aubergine is cooked, it is best if the flesh is salted to bring out excess liquid. Rather than heat up the oven, you could cook the aubergine in a microwave oven; just pierce the skin, wrap in kitchen paper and cook for about 3–4 minutes.

SERVES 4–6
1 aubergine, about 12oz (350g)
salt
1 clove garlic
1 teaspoon fennel seeds
½ teaspoon ground cumin
¼ teaspoon cayenne
½ teaspoon grated fresh root ginger
3 teaspoons tamarind paste (see page 96)
4oz (110g) firm tofu
pepper

Preheat the oven to Gas Mark 4, 350°F (180°C). Roast the aubergine for 20–25 minutes or until quite soft. Slit the aubergine in half lengthwise, sprinkle lightly with salt and leave to drain for 15 minutes.

Meanwhile, pound the garlic with the fennel, cumin, cayenne and ginger in a pestle and mortar to make a rough paste. Mix in the tamarind paste and pound again.

When the aubergine is ready, scrape out the flesh and mash it with the spices. Add the tofu and purée the mixture in a blender or food processor until very smooth. Leave to stand for 2 hours for the flavours to develop. Season to taste before serving.

BAKED PÂTÉS

PINE KERNEL PÂTÉ
WITH MARINATED VEGETABLES

The marinated vegetables in the centre of this nut ring provide a wonderful colour and flavour for the dish as well as adding moisture, rather like serving a nut roast with chutney or relish. It is best to set the vegetables in a very light tomato jelly so that the pâté can be cut in wedges and the vegetables do not collapse. Agar agar is rather unpredictable for setting mousses and soufflés, but it is fine for liquids as long as it is dissolved properly and the liquid is boiled for at least 2 minutes. Serve this pâté at room temperature.

SERVES 4–6
Marinated Vegetables
1 small red pepper
1 small green pepper
6 artichoke hearts, sliced
3 tablespoons olive oil
1 tablespoon red wine vinegar
1 clove garlic, crushed
2 teaspoons herbes de Provence

Pâté

1 tablespoon olive oil
1 onion, peeled and finely chopped
1 clove garlic, crushed
1 tablespoon wholewheat flour
½ pint (275ml) tomato juice
3oz (75g) fresh wholewheat breadcrumbs
2oz (50g) pine kernels, roughly chopped
1oz (25g) ground almonds
1oz (25g) green olives, roughly chopped
2 teaspoons herbes de Provence
2 teaspoons shoyu
1 egg, beaten
salt and pepper
½ teaspoon agar agar
Garnish
extra artichoke hearts, halved, or pine kernels

Preheat the oven to Gas Mark 5, 375°F (190°C). Bake the peppers for 20–30 minutes or until the skin is well charred. Cool slightly, then skin and deseed. Finely chop the flesh. Mix the pepper, artichoke hearts and remaining vegetable ingredients together. Leave to stand for 1–2 hours.

Meanwhile, for the pâté, heat the oil in a pan and lightly cook the onion and garlic for 4–5 minutes until soft. Sprinkle over the flour and cook for 1 minute. Add ¼ pint (150ml) of the tomato juice, and bring to the boil, stirring frequently until smooth.

In a bowl, mix the breadcrumbs, pine kernels, almonds, olives and herbs together. Pour the tomato sauce over the breadcrumb mixture, add the shoyu and egg and mix in well. Season to taste.

Increase the oven temperature to Gas Mark 6, 400°F (200°C). Grease and line a shallow 7-inch (18-cm) ring mould. Layer the extra artichoke hearts or pine kernels for the garnish in the bottom. Cover with the nut pâté, pressing down well. Bake for 50 minutes or until quite firm. Allow to cool slightly before turning out.

Finally, drain the marinated vegetables and pile them into the centre of the pâté. Any remaining vegetables can be arranged around the outside. Dissolve the agar agar into the remaining tomato juice. Bring to the boil and simmer for 2 minutes. Check the setting property by dropping a tiny amount onto a cold surface and seeing if it gels. Pour the liquid over the marinated vegetables in the centre of the pâté. Use just enough to cover them. Leave to set. Serve the pâté in wedges.

LEEK AND MUSHROOM RAMEKINS

Photograph on page 34

Once you have tried these two vegetable purées, you can experiment with others – cauliflower, broccoli and spinach work well, as do peppers provided they are roasted and skinned first. Root vegetables such as celeriac, carrot and parsnip are also worth using.

SERVES 4
Leek Filling
¾oz (20g) sunflower margarine
¾oz (20g) wholewheat flour
¼ pint (150ml) vegetable stock
2 teaspoons mild mustard
1 tablespoon capers, chopped
12oz (350g) leeks, cleaned and diced
1 egg
salt and pepper
Mushroom Filling
1 tablespoon sunflower oil
8oz (225g) button mushrooms
1 clove garlic
2 sticks of celery, very finely chopped
4oz (110g) feta cheese
1 egg

Preheat the oven to Gas Mark 4, 350°F (180°C). Melt the margarine in a pan, add the flour and cook for 1 minute, stirring, until smooth. Pour in the stock and add the mustard and capers. Bring to the boil, stirring, and simmer for 2–3 minutes.

Steam the leeks for 4 minutes. Purée with the sauce in a blender or food processor until completely smooth. Cool slightly, then beat in the egg and season to taste.

For the mushroom layer, heat the oil in a pan and gently cook the mushrooms, garlic and celery for 4–5 minutes or until quite soft. Purée with the feta cheese in a blender or food processor. Cool slightly, then beat in the egg and season to taste. Chill both mixtures well.

Grease 4 ramekin dishes and line the bases with greaseproof paper. Spoon in alternate layers of leek and mushroom filling – there should be 2 layers of each. Place the dishes in a bain-marie. Bake for 45–50 minutes. Cool, then turn out.

SNACKS &
SAVOURIES

It is useful to have a range of these ideas on hand as they solve all sorts of mealtime problems, such as what to offer for a cooked breakfast, how to make a quick lunch, a healthy high tea or light late-night suppers that won't keep you awake until the small hours. Remember that the trend towards lighter eating should not mean that the food is dull, lacking in imagination, flavour or nutrients. In this chapter I deal with making savouries on toast, give ideas for meals with eggs, show you a range of burgers and give specific recipes for cocktail savouries.

SNACKS ON TOAST

Tasty toppings for toast include a classic Welsh Rarebit, popular Marinated Mushrooms and an unusual Tofu Scramble. Don't forget that the toast is the basis of these snacks and variations in the kind of bread you use will make the meal more interesting. All the recipes in the chapter on bread and cereals, apart from the brioche, could be used as a foil for your choice of topping. Otherwise use a pitta bread or Indian-style pancake such as the Cumin Pancakes on page 107.

A nutritious topping, especially one that includes beans, nuts, dairy products or tofu, on a wholesome base can be a healthy and sustaining meal. Try different toast toppings, such as slices of pâté or some of the spreads from the previous chapter. A portion of Mexican Beans (page 115) on toast makes a welcome change from the classic baked bean.

WELSH RAREBIT

Traditional cheese on toast should not be ignored as a quick snack, but it is worth adding one or two extra ingredients to make a more interesting meal. In the north, there is the tradition of adding beer or ale to the cheese. I like using cider, but if you haven't any to hand, a little concentrated apple juice and cider vinegar work very well. Make toppings more tasty with a few spicy additions or finely chopped vegetables and try other breads.

SERVES 1
¼oz (7g) butter
1 tablespoon dry cider
1 teaspoon mustard with creamed horseradish or ½ teaspoon prepared mustard and ½ teaspoon creamed horseradish
2oz (50g) Cheddar cheese, finely grated
2 slices of wholewheat bread

Beat the butter, cider, mustard and horseradish into the cheese in a bowl.

Toast the bread on one side. Spread the cheese mixture over the other side and toast until golden brown.

MARINATED MUSHROOMS

Use field mushrooms for this recipe if you intend to serve them on toast for a supper or breakfast dish. For savouries, it is best to choose very small button mushrooms, which can be left whole, and serve them on a savoury biscuit or with other vegetables on a cocktail stick.

SERVES 2–4
2 tablespoons olive oil
8oz (225g) button mushrooms, left whole or field mushrooms, thickly sliced
2 tablespoons red wine
1 red chilli, deseeded and diced
2–3 cloves garlic
6 green peppercorns, diced
2 spring onions, trimmed and chopped
1 teaspoon shoyu
pepper

Heat a little of the oil and lightly fry the mushrooms for 3 minutes until just softened. This will help them absorb more dressing.

Mix the remaining ingredients for the marinade together, pour over the hot mushrooms and stir well. Cover and leave for several hours or overnight. Drain well before serving on toast, savoury biscuits or cocktail sticks.

LOW-FAT WELSH RAREBIT

SERVES 1
1oz (25g) Cheddar cheese, finely grated
1oz (25g) cottage cheese
4–5 drops Tabasco sauce
2 slices of wholewheat bread
1 tomato, sliced

Beat the first 3 ingredients together in a bowl.

Toast the bread on one side. Spread the cheese mixture over the other side, cover with slices of tomato and toast until golden brown.

TOFU SCRAMBLE

This makes an extremely delicious, quick nutritious snack for one person – simply multiply the amounts if you need to make more. Tofu readily absorbs flavours. This recipe is mildly spiced, but you could get a different flavour using fresh herbs. For a more substantial snack, gently cook some finely chopped mushrooms or peppers, then scramble the tofu into these. Keep the oil used to a minimum to avoid a greasy aftertaste.

SERVES 1
1–2 teaspoons sunflower oil
3 spring onions, trimmed and chopped
¼ teaspoon turmeric
pinch of cumin
pinch of chilli powder
4oz (110g) firm tofu, roughly chopped
2 teaspoons shoyu
sesame salt (gomasio) and pepper

Heat the oil in a frying pan and gently cook the spring onions for 3–4 minutes. Add the spices and cook for 1 minute, stirring well.

Add the tofu and cook for about 5–7 minutes, stirring constantly. This will break down the tofu to a scramble consistency and also reduce the liquid. Add the shoyu and season to taste. Serve hot on slices of toast or in a baked potato.

MEALS WITH EGGS

I haven't included many specifically egg recipes in this book as we are all familiar with the classic omelette and soufflé, and the numerous other popular ways of preparing eggs. Eggs and cheese, which are so versatile, are often the first things that people turn to when trying to eat less meat. However, I realise that changing to a wholefood diet, using more pulses, grains and nuts, takes time, and there are many occasions when eggs can fill a gap.

BAKED OMELETTE

I once watched a Spanish chef flip over a twelve-egg omelette laden with potatoes and onion in the pan. After my own disastrous attempt, he kindly explained that it took a great deal of practice! This dish is rather like a Spanish omelette, but as it is baked in the oven, it saves you the problem of trying to turn the omelette over. You are not restricted to potatoes, tomatoes and peas; other vegetables, fresh or cooked left-overs, can easily be used instead. Make sure that you have a colourful, well flavoured mixture.

SERVES 2
8oz (225g) boiled potatoes, thickly sliced
2 large tomatoes, skinned and sliced
1 onion, peeled and diced
4oz (110g) peas
3 tablespoons olive or sunflower oil
4 eggs
1 teaspoon dried oregano
1 teaspoon dried thyme
salt and pepper

Preheat the oven to Gas Mark 4, 350°F (180°C). Layer the vegetables in an oiled shallow ovenproof dish and pour the oil over the top. Bake for 20 minutes.

Beat the eggs thoroughly, whisk in the herbs and season well. Pour the eggs over the baked vegetables. Bake for a further 20 minutes or until the eggs have completely set. Serve immediately.

CHINESE STYLE OMELETTE

This style of filling is rather like a spring roll with the beansprouts and mushrooms. It works particularly well in an omelette, providing a contrast in texture and a good flavour. The very thin omelettes made in the Far East are usually cooked in a wok, but it takes a little practice to get them right. An omelette pan can be used instead, but keep the omelette as thin as possible. The end result should be lighter than a traditional omelette, but just as satisfying.

SERVES 1–2
Filling
2 teaspoons peanut oil
2 spring onions, trimmed and diced
1 clove garlic, crushed
2oz (50g) firm tofu, cubed
2oz (50g) beansprouts
2oz (50g) mushrooms, wiped and thinly sliced
1 tablespoon shoyu
Omelette
2 eggs
2 tablespoons water
pinch of salt
1 tablespoon dry sherry
Garnish
fresh coriander sprigs or spring onions

For the filling, heat the oil in a wok or large frying pan and stir fry the spring onions for 30 seconds. Stir in the garlic, then add the tofu, beansprouts and mushrooms and stir fry for 2 minutes over a high heat. Mix in the shoyu. Set the filling aside.

For the omelette, beat the eggs and water together thoroughly and add the salt. Use either a wok or an omelette pan to make a large very thin omelette. If you are using the wok, the mixture should be thin enough to cook through without turning it over. In a traditional pan, you may need to turn the omelette over after 2–3 minutes.

When cooked, pile on the stir-fry filling and roll up or fold the omelette over. Slide on to a warm plate. Quickly pour the sherry into the pan and heat until just boiling. Spoon the sherry over the omelette, garnish and serve straight away.

SUNFLOWER SOUFFLÉS

Photograph on page 67

Soufflés make a marvellous starter to a meal, or a light main course served with salad and following a substantial soup. Impressive as a large soufflé is, individual ones are just as simple to make and easier to serve. Usually it is not worth attempting them for unpunctual guests, however this idea is a little different as the soufflé is actually allowed to become cold, coated in a nutty mixture of wheatgerm and sunflower seeds, then briefly reheated. The result is more like a light, puffy cake, with an excellent flavour. Do use a strong tasting cheese (I have found a particularly good vegetarian Edam). Use cornmeal for the sauce as it is light and gives the soufflés a golden colour. For a more substantial dish, fold a few cooked, chopped vegetables into the white sauce.

SERVES 4

½oz (15g) sunflower margarine
½oz (15g) fine cornmeal
4fl oz (110ml) skimmed milk
3oz (75g) Edam cheese, grated
1 egg, separated
2 teaspoons orange juice
pepper
1½ tablespoons sunflower seeds
1 tablespoon wheatgerm

Preheat the oven to Gas Mark 6, 400°F (200°C). Melt the margarine in a pan, stir in the cornmeal and cook for 1 minute. Add the milk, bring to the boil, stirring frequently, then simmer for 1 minute.

Cool slightly, then add the cheese and egg yolk. Stir in the orange juice. Whisk the egg white until stiff but not dry, then fold into the mixture. Season to taste.

Divide the soufflé mixture between 4 greased ramekin dishes. Place in a bain-marie. Bake for 10–12 minutes. As they cool, they will flatten. When cold, turn them out.

Grind 1 tablespoon of the sunflower seeds finely in a nut mill or coffee grinder and mix with the wheatgerm. Coat the soufflés in the mixture. Chop the remaining sunflower seeds coarsely, sprinkle over the tops and, just before serving, reheat in the oven for 4–6 minutes.

BURGERS & CROQUETTES

Burgers as snacks and meals are enormously successful as shown by the ever present high street takeaways and snack bars. Even these havens for meat eaters are now being invaded by vegetarian burgers, based on mixtures of nuts, cereals and generous amounts of herbs and spices. I am sure their popularity will increase once people have tried them.

Home-made burgers can be served in the classic style with a (preferably) wholewheat bun, chutney sauce and a crisp salad. Alternatively, bake burgers in a tomato sauce and serve with plain brown rice, or another grain dish like Fruity Barley on page 93. Make miniature burgers and croquettes as cocktail savouries or as part of a buffet spread.

There are plenty of ways you can experiment with burgers using the different flavours and textures of herbs and spices and cooked or raw vegetables. Grains, pulses and nuts form the base of burger and croquette recipes. Mixes such as these will benefit from being left to stand so that the flavours can develop. If the mixture is too moist, add cereals such as oatflakes or wholewheat breadcrumbs to thicken but be careful not to make the end result too heavy. An egg or a tablespoon of tahini and a little stock will help bind loose ingredients together for easier frying.

Serve burgers with a cold sauce or dip such as Spiced Yoghurt (page 92) or Cottage Cheese Dressing (page 179) or use a thin spreading of Red Pepper and Sunflower Dip (page 50) or Courgette and Cheese Dip (page 49), or a more substantial hot sauce or casserole like the Marinated Vegetable Sauce on page 75.

BULGAR WHEAT CROQUETTES

Bulgar wheat comes from the whole wheat grain, which is steamed and cracked. Because it is partially cooked in processing, bulgar wheat is extremely quick to use. Once cooked, the texture is light and the flavour nutty. All grains can be enhanced with a range of herbs and spices. As bulgar wheat is so popular in Middle Eastern cuisine, I have used the fragrant flavours of cumin and coriander in this recipe. The trick with making croquettes from grains, such as rice or wheat, is to stir them well as they cook. This releases the gluten and makes them very sticky. Once cooled, you can mix in the other ingredients and easily shape the mixture into burgers or croquettes, and they shouldn't fall apart in the pan. Make small patties for party savouries and larger croquettes as a main course. Serve with a sharp-flavoured yoghurt-based sauce or dip.

MAKES 16–20

6oz (175g) bulgar wheat
½ teaspoon salt
12fl oz (350ml) boiling water
1oz (25g) sesame seeds
1 tablespoon olive oil
1 onion, peeled and finely chopped
3–4 tablespoons finely chopped fresh coriander
1 teaspoon ground cumin
1–2 tablespoons lemon juice
1 tablespoon shoyu
pepper
sunflower oil for shallow frying

Mix the bulgar wheat and salt together in a bowl. Pour over the boiling water and leave to soak for 20 minutes.

Toast the sesame seeds either under the grill or in a dry frying pan for 3–4 minutes until lightly browned. Coarsely grind in a pestle and mortar.

Heat the oil in a pan and gently cook the onion for 5–7 minutes until soft and translucent. Add the soaked bulgar wheat and sesame seeds, stirring well. Cook for 5–7 minutes, stirring frequently so that the grain becomes quite sticky. Add the coriander, cumin, lemon juice and shoyu and cook for a further 2–3 minutes. Leave to cool, then season to taste.

Shape the grain mixture into small balls. Shallow fry in a little oil for 3–4 minutes on each side until golden brown. Drain on kitchen paper. Serve hot.

TOASTED NUT BURGERS

This very simple recipe is made successful by using a good stock, fresh herbs and toasted nuts, all of which give the burgers an excellent taste. I like to use a mixture of creamy nuts such as cashews and Brazils as well as the more robust hazelnut and walnut. Peanuts can be added to give a drier flavour and for economy's sake. Add finely chopped cooked mushrooms, celery or peppers and generous amounts of fresh herbs to this recipe to ring the changes.

SERVES 4

1 tablespoon sunflower oil
1 onion, peeled and finely chopped
1 clove garlic, crushed
4oz (110g) mixed nuts
4oz (110g) fresh wholewheat breadcrumbs
2 tablespoons chopped fresh parsley
¼ pint (150ml) vegetable stock
1 egg
2 teaspoons shoyu
salt and pepper
sunflower oil for shallow frying
Coating (optional)
1 egg, beaten
2–3oz (50–75g) fresh wholewheat breadcrumbs

Preheat the oven to Gas Mark 4, 350°F (180°C). Heat the oil in a pan and gently fry the onion for 4–5 minutes until soft. Add the garlic and cook for 1 minute. Toast the nuts in the oven for 10–15 minutes, then coarsely chop.

Mix the toasted nuts and breadcrumbs together in a large bowl. Add the cooked onion mixture, the parsley and enough stock to moisten the ingredients thoroughly. Mix in the egg, then add the shoyu and season to taste. Leave to stand if possible for 2 hours.

Shape the mixture into burgers or rissoles and coat in egg and breadcrumbs if liked. Shallow fry for 3–4 minutes on each side before serving.

LENTIL AND WALNUT BURGERS

Most pulses, once cooked and ground or mashed, make a good base for a burger as they are quite floury in texture and will also hold together well. Flavour with nuts, herbs and spices, alternatively use very finely chopped cooked vegetables, as these give moisture and colour. Seasonings such as yeast extracts, miso, shoyu or ketchups are extremely useful to provide more taste. I also find that a small quantity of lemon juice or vinegar counteracts the dryness of the mashed beans. Try to make the basic mixture in advance, so that the flavours have a chance to develop. Burgers should be shallow fried unless otherwise directed. They are not really successful deep fried because the mixture can disintegrate. If you want to avoid frying, bake the burgers in the oven, but remember the end result will be slightly drier. You can solve this problem by baking them in a sauce.

MAKES 8
6oz (175g) brown lentils
1 tablespoon olive oil
1 small onion, peeled and diced
1 clove garlic
¼ teaspoon ground turmeric
¼ teaspoon ground cumin
¼ teaspoon ground ginger
juice of ½ lemon
2 tablespoons natural yoghurt
2oz (50g) walnuts, finely chopped
2oz (50g) fine oatmeal
salt and pepper
sunflower oil for shallow frying

Pick over the lentils for stones, then rinse and drain thoroughly. Place the lentils in a large pan of water and simmer for 25–30 minutes or until well cooked. Drain well and set aside.

Heat the oil in a pan and gently cook the onion and garlic for 3–4 minutes or until just softened. Add the spices and cook for 2 minutes. Mix the cooked onion and spices with the lentils. Add the lemon juice, yoghurt, nuts and oatmeal. Leave to stand for about 30 minutes to allow the mixture time to firm up.

Season the mixture and shape into 8 burgers. Shallow fry the burgers in a little oil for 4–5 minutes on each side. Serve hot or warm with a sauce, dip or relish.

COCKTAIL SAVOURIES

Serve these appetisers before a meal or as part of a selection for a finger food supper. It is certainly an easy way to entertain if all the food can be eaten without a knife and fork but do remember that a lot of small dishes will take time to prepare.

Other nibbles to offer at this sort of occasion are plain toasted nuts or seeds (or toss them lightly in a little shoyu); olives, especially the large purple-black Kalamata variety; crudités; savoury biscuits or thin slices of bread topped with a spread.

STUFFED TOMATOES

Tomatoes make a colourful addition to any buffet spread. They can be filled with a variety of mixtures, including the bean pâtés on pages 45–8. Here, well-flavoured tofu is the basic ingredient.

FILLS 16 CHERRY TOMATOES

16 cherry tomatoes
1 tablespoon sesame or sunflower seeds
4oz (110g) firm tofu
2 tablespoons finely chopped fresh parsley
1 spring onion, finely chopped, or
1 tablespoon finely chopped chives
¼ teaspoon celery seeds
1 teaspoon sesame or walnut oil
salt
Garnish
extra toasted seeds or chopped fresh parsley

Slice a lid from the base of each tomato and hollow out the inside.

Lightly toast the seeds under the grill or in a microwave oven at full power for 2–3 minutes. Coarsely crush in a pestle and mortar.

Blend the tofu with the crushed seeds and remaining ingredients until light and smooth. Leave to stand for 2–3 hours or overnight. Season to taste. Fill each tomato with a little of the filling. Garnish with extra toasted seeds or chopped parsley.

Opposite: Sunflower Soufflés (page 61) and Fruit Kebabs (page 70)

STUFFED DATES

Fresh dates have become more readily available and they are easy to fill and look very attractive. This recipe could also be part of a dessert platter of fruit and nuts.

FILLS 24 DATES
2oz (50g) cashew nuts
1 tablespoon creamy peanut butter
2 tablespoons curd cheese or quark
1 medium apple, peeled, cored and finely grated
salt and pepper
24 fresh dates

Preheat the oven to Gas Mark 5, 375°F (190°C). Toast the nuts in the oven for 5–10 minutes until lightly browned. Alternatively, toast in a microwave oven at full power for 2 minutes. Finely grind in a nut mill or coffee grinder. Mix in the peanut butter, curd cheese and apple. Season to taste. Stone the dates and spoon a little filling into each cavity.

SPICED CASHEW NUTS WITH CHILLI

It is always worth toasting nuts when you serve them as a snack as the flavour is vastly improved. Here chilli and paprika give colour and spice, balanced with fresh coriander and lemon juice. This idea also makes a crunchy accompaniment for topping a casserole or curry.

SERVES 4
6oz (175g) cashew nuts
1 green chilli, deseeded and finely chopped
½ teaspoon paprika
2 tablespoons finely chopped fresh coriander
1 tablespoon lemon juice
small lemon wedges for serving

Preheat the oven to Gas Mark 5, 375°F (190°C). Toast the cashew nuts in the oven for 5–10 minutes or under the grill until lightly browned.

Toss the nuts with the chilli, paprika and coriander. Just before serving, stir in the lemon juice. Serve with wedges of lemon.

Opposite: Wholewheat tagliatelle with Leek and Mushroom Sauce (page 76)

FRUIT KEBABS

Photograph on page 67

Colourful kebabs of fruit make a light and attractive starter to a substantial meal, or they could be served as part of a main course with salads and Cottage Cheese Dressing (page 179). You can use all sorts of different fruits to make attractive arrangements. Summer fruits such as strawberries, peaches and apricots all work well, or try the autumnal plums and greengages for a change. Remember to choose fruits whose colour will not spoil by being exposed to the air. Apples, pears and bananas are all unsuitable for this reason. For an appetiser or a buffet party make miniature kebabs, using cocktail sticks.

SERVES 4
8oz (225g) grapes
1 ogen melon
2 satsumas
4oz (110g) strawberries
8 mint leaves
crisp lettuce or chicory leaves for serving
Sauce
juice of ½ orange
1 teaspoon grated orange rind
1 tablespoon lemon juice
3 teaspoons clear honey
2 teaspoons sunflower oil
½ teaspoon arrowroot
1 teaspoon poppy seeds

For the sauce, mix all the ingredients, except the poppy seeds, together in a small pan. Bring to the boil, stirring well, and simmer for 2 minutes until the sauce thickens and clears. Remove from the heat and stir in the poppy seeds. Leave the sauce to cool while preparing the fruit.

Deseed the grapes if necessary. Cut the melon in half, deseed and scoop the flesh into balls. Peel and segment the satsumas. Remove the stalks from the strawberries.

Toss all the fruit in the sauce and leave for up to 1 hour. Slide the fruit on to long kebab skewers in an attractive pattern, adding the mint leaves. Alternatively, place each kebab in a boat-shaped container made from lettuce or chicory leaves. Serve chilled, with the sauce in a separate bowl.

PASTA

Pasta is the Italian word for dough, traditionally made from hard or durum wheat. The plainest dough is made with flour, salt and water; richer doughs include olive oil or eggs which also make the dough more filling. Variations with flavours include most frequently a spinach purée or a tomato paste. Dried wholewheat pasta has been readily available in wholefood shops for some time now and is a useful addition to any store cupboard as it can provide quick, simple meals. Store in a dry place and it will keep for several months. Fresh pasta is now increasingly popular and available. It is lighter than dried pasta but does need using within two to three days of purchase. There is still a rather limited choice of fresh wholewheat pasta. However, it is quite easy to make your own (page 80) with a little practice and some experience of wholewheat dough.

Wholewheat pasta is a good source of protein and a way of making extremely quick and sustaining meals. A freshly cooked, piping hot pasta with a well flavoured sauce, accompanied or preceded by salad and followed with a light pudding such as Ricotta Cheesecake (page 220) or Pineapple Sorbet (page 218), can make a splendid meal. None of the pasta sauces take much preparation. Others to experiment with are the Cream Cheese Sauce for gnocchi on page 99 or Cheese and Chilli Sauce for polenta on page 100. You can use a variety of pasta shapes with these sauces – spaghetti, tagliatelle, fettucine, capellini (angel hair) or trenette.

Baked pasta dishes, such as lasagne and macaroni, take a little more preparation but make satisfying and appealing main courses.

Pasta isn't exclusive to Italy. Similar ideas are used in many Far Eastern cuisines – principally noodles which are made from wheat, rice or bean flour. A variety known as Soba is a Japanese buckwheat noodle, the equivalent of spaghetti. These types of pastas are generally available dried. Experiment and mix and match different sauces with different pastas or noodles to create your own unique dishes.

As a rule of thumb, the thinner or more delicate the pasta, the lighter the accompanying sauce. Thin smooth sauces, or the simplest mixture of herbs, garlic and oil such as pesto can be tossed in just before serving; chunkier sauces such as the marinated vegetables should be piled on top. More substantial pasta such as lasagne or large tubes of cannelloni will hold substantial fillings made with vegetable purée, cheese sauce or nuts.

My macaroni recipe uses soya milk as its creamy, nutty flavour gives an extra dimension to this classic dish – although a dish to be enjoyed by everyone it is a useful recipe for vegans and those allergic to dairy products.

Apart from all these mouthwatering meals, don't forget that cold pasta makes a good base for a substantial salad such as Pasta and Chick Pea (page 184) – the twists, shells and wheat ear shapes look particularly attractive. You can also add pasta, especially the short cut varieties such as penne, farfalle (bow-ties), fucilli and macaroni, to soups and casseroles to make them more sustaining, as in the classic minestrone soup.

Cooking pasta
Cooking pasta is easy and very quick so make sure your family or guests are ready to eat as there is nothing worse than overcooked or tepid pasta. Allow 4–5oz (110–150g) per person when serving pastas such as spaghetti or tagliatelle as a main course, use 2–3oz (50–75g) for a starter. With more substantial pastas, such as lasagne, use a little less. Always use plenty of water so the pasta has enough room to swell up and won't stick together. About 4 pints (2.25 litres) is sufficient for 8oz (225g) pasta. Add a little salt and a few drops of olive oil to the boiling water. Add the pasta to the boiling water and bring back to the boil again very quickly, then simmer until cooked. Cooking times vary according to whether the pasta is fresh or dried. Fresh unfilled pastas take 3–4 minutes or 8–12 minutes if dried. Fresh filled pasta takes 8–10 minutes or 12–15 minutes if dried. To test if pasta is cooked, remove a piece; if you can bite through it and there is a little resistance, then it is 'al dente' and ready.

Once cooked, drain the pasta well and serve immediately on warmed plates – shallow soup plates are most useful as they hold the heat well and also the sauce!

If you have cold left-over pasta, particularly the short cut varieties, use in salads or toss in a little oil and heat through in a microwave oven.

PARSLEY PESTO

Traditional Italian pesto uses ground pine kernels, olive oil, garlic and plenty of fresh basil to provide an extremely rich and creamy sauce. It can be added to soups, sauces and casseroles to give a subtle herb undertone, or simply tossed with freshly cooked pasta for an easy but delicious supper dish or starter. Unfortunately it is not always possible to obtain fresh basil and the dried version of this herb does not produce the same effect. By experimenting with the basic principle, I have found you can make good herb sauces using fresh parsley or coriander, and still retain the overall creamy effect because of the ground nuts.

SERVES 4
2oz (50g) pine kernels
2 cloves garlic, crushed
2 tablespoons olive oil
2–3 tablespoons finely chopped fresh parsley
1 teaspoon dried marjoram
salt and pepper

Crush the pine kernels with the remaining ingredients in a pestle and mortar or blender to make a smooth paste. Adjust the quantities if you prefer more garlic or oil for example. Season to taste. Store in a screwtop jar in the refrigerator.

WALNUT PESTO

This recipe has a stronger flavour than Parsley Pesto due to the robust taste of walnuts. Do be sure to buy fresh looking nuts.

SERVES 4
2oz (50g) walnuts
2 cloves garlic, crushed
2 tablespoons olive oil
2–3 tablespoons finely chopped fresh coriander
1–2 tablespoons finely chopped fresh mint
salt and pepper

Crush the walnuts with the remaining ingredients in a pestle and mortar or blender to make a smooth paste. Season to taste. Store in a screwtop jar in the refrigerator.

MARINATED VEGETABLE SAUCE

This is a chunky sauce that could be served with pasta spirals or macaroni, or as a side vegetable with a pasty. It is also excellent as a pancake
filling and can even be served cold.

SERVES 4

3 large red, yellow or green peppers
6 tablespoons olive oil
6oz (175g) aubergine, cut into large chunks
2 tablespoons red wine vinegar
1 clove garlic, sliced
1 red chilli, deseeded and diced
1 tablespoon dried oregano
1 tablespoon chopped fresh basil
1½lb (700g) courgettes, trimmed and diced
2 tablespoons finely chopped fresh parsley
8oz (225g) pasta shells, freshly cooked

Preheat the oven to Gas Mark 6, 400°F (200°C). Bake the peppers
(turning them over once during baking) for 25–30 minutes. The skins
should be quite charred and easy to remove. Skin, then slice the flesh.

Heat 2 tablespoons of the oil in a pan and lightly fry the aubergine.
Remove from the heat and add the remaining oil and the vinegar, garlic,
chilli, oregano and basil. Transfer to a bowl and mix in the sliced
peppers. Cover and chill overnight.

Next day, steam the courgettes for 4–6 minutes or until just tender.
Mix them into the marinated vegetables with the parsley. Put into a pan
and cook over a low heat until heated through.

Toss freshly cooked pasta into the hot vegetables and serve
immediately.

LEEK AND MUSHROOM SAUCE

Photograph on page 68

SERVES 4

1 tablespoon olive oil
8oz (225g) leeks, cleaned and sliced
12oz (350g) button mushrooms, wiped
1 red pepper, deseeded and diced
1 × 14oz (400g) tin of tomatoes, puréed
1 tablespoon tomato purée
2–3 tablespoons traditional or Parsley pesto (page 74)
1 teaspoon miso

Heat the oil in a pan and gently cook the leeks for 4–5 minutes. If the mushrooms are small, keep them whole, but otherwise slice thickly. Stir in the mushrooms and red pepper and cook for 3 minutes. Stir in the tomatoes and tomato purée, bring to the boil, cover and simmer for 25 minutes. Add the pesto, mix in well and continue cooking, uncovered, for 20 minutes. Dissolve the miso in a little of the sauce, then mix in. Serve the sauce hot with freshly cooked pasta.

LENTIL SAUCE

This sauce has a sweet and sour flavour.

SERVES 4

2oz (50g) dried apricots
2oz (50g) red lentils
1 pint (570ml) water
2–3 tablespoons shoyu
1 tablespoon white wine vinegar
pinch of aniseed
salt and pepper

Finely slice the apricots using kitchen scissors. Rinse the lentils thoroughly.

Put the apricots and lentils in a medium pan and pour over the water. Bring to the boil, cover and simmer for 20–25 minutes or until the lentils are well softened. Cool slightly, then purée in a blender or food processor until smooth. Add the shoyu, wine vinegar and aniseed to taste. Season well, then reheat slightly and serve with freshly cooked pasta.

CASHEW AND GINGER SAUCE

Puréed fennel and cashew nuts make this sauce very creamy. Serve with pasta spirals or tagliatelli.

SERVES 4
2 tablespoons olive oil
7oz (200g) fennel, finely chopped
½ teaspoon fennel seeds
2oz (50g) cashew nuts
½ teaspoon grated fresh root ginger
½ pint (275ml) vegetable stock
salt and pepper
12oz (350g) French beans, trimmed and thickly sliced

Heat the oil in a pan and gently cook the fennel for 7–10 minutes. Add the fennel seeds and mix well.

Lightly toast the cashew nuts under the grill or in a dry frying pan for about 1 minute to bring out the flavour. Do not let them colour, or the colour of the sauce will be spoiled. Grind half the cashew nuts in a nut mill or coffee grinder, reserving the remaining pieces.

Add the ground cashew nuts and ginger to the fennel, stir well and cook for 1 minute. Pour over the stock, bring to the boil, cover and simmer for 10 minutes. Cool slightly, then purée in a blender or food processor until smooth. Season to taste.

Steam the French beans for 4–5 minutes or until just tender. Toss the beans and whole cashew nuts into the sauce. Mix into freshly cooked pasta and serve straight away.

LASAGNE WITH NUT AND WINE SAUCE

There are many variations on the theme of lasagne for serving as every-day suppers or dinner parties. I always find it is a popular dish and very easy to present well. This particular recipe is probably more suitable for special occasions as the sauce filling is rich with wine and walnuts. Both these ingredients add a distinctive strong flavour and colour. Coarsely chop the walnuts to add texture: if you grind them, you may find they become too oily. If you do not want to make your own pasta, there are several varieties you can buy. One type is pre-cooked, which saves one stage when assembling this recipe.

SERVES 4

6oz (175g) lasagne
Nut and Wine Sauce
1 tablespoon olive oil
1 onion, peeled and finely chopped
1 clove garlic
1 red or green pepper, deseeded and diced
3 sticks of celery, trimmed and diced
8oz (225g) French beans, trimmed and diced
1 × 14oz (400g) tin of tomatoes, puréed
2 tablespoons tomato purée
1 teaspoon dried marjoram or basil
2 tablespoons pesto (page 74)
¼ pint (150ml) red wine
2oz (50g) walnuts, coarsely chopped
salt and pepper
Cheese Sauce
1½oz (40g) sunflower margarine
1½oz (40g) wholewheat flour
1 pint (570ml) milk, infused with ½ onion, parsley sprig and 1 bay leaf
4oz (110g) cheese, grated
pinch of mustard powder

For the nut and wine sauce, heat the oil in a pan and gently cook the onion and garlic for 4–5 minutes. Add the pepper, celery and beans to the pan, stir in well and cook for 5 minutes. Stir in the tomatoes, tomato purée, marjoram, pesto, wine and walnuts. Bring to the boil and simmer, uncovered, for 40 minutes. Season to taste.

Meanwhile, for the cheese sauce, melt the margarine in a pan over a gentle heat. Sprinkle on the flour and stir well. Cook the roux for 1 minute, stirring. Gradually add the milk, a third at a time, stirring in thoroughly until smooth. Bring to the boil and simmer for 3–4 minutes, stirring. Remove the pan from the heat, add half the grated cheese and the mustard powder.

Preheat the oven to Gas Mark 4, 350°F (180°C). Cook the lasagne in plenty of boiling salted water for 8 minutes or until just softened. Drain.

To assemble the lasagne, put a little of the nut and wine sauce in the base of a greased ovenproof dish. Cover with a layer of lasagne, then coat with some cheese sauce. Repeat these layers, ending with cheese sauce. Scatter the remaining cheese on top. Bake for 20–25 minutes. Serve hot.

CREAMED MACARONI AND VEGETABLES

This recipe is lighter than the traditional macaroni cheese as it is made with vegetables and nuts. As a variation, I have used soya milk for the sauce, which is an easy way to introduce this versatile ingredient.

SERVES 4
¾ pint (450ml) soya milk
¼ pint (150ml) water
½ onion, peeled
1 bay leaf
6 peppercorns
2oz (50g) sunflower margarine
2oz (50g) wholewheat flour
1 teaspoon prepared mustard
2 tablespoons yeast flakes
2oz (50g) ground walnuts
salt
8oz (225g) macaroni or small pasta shapes
12oz (350g) broccoli, divided in florets
8oz (225g) carrots, peeled and diced
2oz (50g) walnuts, chopped
1–2oz (25–50g) fresh wholewheat breadcrumbs

For the sauce, dilute the soya milk with the water in a pan. Add the onion, bay leaf and peppercorns and bring to boiling point. Leave to stand for 10 minutes, then strain.

Melt the margarine in a medium pan, sprinkle over the flour and stir to make a roux. Cook for 1 minute, then gradually add the soya milk, stirring constantly. Bring to the boil and simmer for 2 minutes, stirring. Remove the pan from the heat and add the mustard, yeast flakes and walnuts. Season to taste.

Bring a large pan of water to the boil. When boiling fast, add a little salt and oil, then stir in the macaroni. Simmer for 8–10 minutes.

Meanwhile, lightly steam the vegetables until just tender. Finally, mix the sauce, pasta and vegetables together. Spoon into a greased flameproof serving dish and top with the walnuts and breadcrumbs. Grill for 5 minutes to toast the nuts before serving.

FRESH PASTA DISHES

It is necessary to make your own pasta dough for home-made ravioli, and you can use it also for lasagne, canneloni or tagliatelle. Fresh pasta is not difficult to make by hand, especially once you get accustomed to the feel of wholewheat dough.

FRESH WHOLEWHEAT PASTA

In making fresh wholemeal pasta, always err on the side of making wetter dough as, when resting, the fibres in the flour will expand and excess water will be absorbed. You can always add a little extra flour when rolling out the dough. A pasta-making machine certainly helps you obtain a thinner dough. If you are rolling out by hand, do be patient and roll it as thin as possible. As wholewheat dough is invariably more substantial, I prefer to make it richer by adding eggs. This makes it more tasty than versions just made with water. Semolina helps keep the mixture lighter. Make flavoured pastas by adding herbs or tomato purée to the basic mixture. If you like green pasta, add a spinach purée, but reduce the amount of water added.

MAKES 1½LB (700G) PASTA

14oz (400g) wholewheat flour

2oz (50g) semolina

pinch of salt

2 eggs, beaten

4–5fl oz (100–150ml) cold water

Mix the flour, semolina and salt together in a large bowl. Add the eggs to the flour with enough water to make a smooth dough. Draw up the ingredients to form a ball, then knead the mixture well until quite elastic.

Leave the dough to rest for 30 minutes before rolling out and using.

CANNELONI WITH SPICED YOGHURT AND TOMATO SAUCE

This spicy lentil stuffing blends Italian and Middle Eastern cuisines.

SERVES 4
1 quantity Fresh Wholewheat Pasta (page 80)
Filling
4oz (110g) continental lentils
2oz (50g) sunflower seeds
2 tablespoons olive oil
1 onion, peeled and finely chopped
2 cloves garlic
8oz (225g) courgettes, trimmed and diced
8oz (225g) field mushrooms, chopped
1 teaspoon garam masala
2 tablespoons chopped fresh coriander
1 tablespoon chopped fresh mint
1 tablespoon cider vinegar
salt and pepper
Sauce
2 tablespoons olive oil
1 onion, peeled and finely chopped
1 clove garlic, crushed
1 tablespoon wholewheat flour
1 × 14oz (400g) tin of tomatoes, mashed
1 bay leaf
4 tablespoons natural yoghurt
1 tablespoon chopped fresh coriander leaves
1 teaspoon cider vinegar
salt and pepper
2oz (50g) toasted sunflower seeds for serving

Pick over the lentils for stones, then rinse well. Place in a pan with plenty of fresh water and add the sunflower seeds. Bring to the boil, cover and simmer for 35–40 minutes until the lentils are tender. Drain well.

Heat the oil in a large pan and gently fry the onion and garlic for 4–5 minutes or until soft. Add the courgettes, mushrooms and garam masala. Mix well, then cook for 9–10 minutes. Stir in the cooked lentils and sunflower seeds, coriander, mint and vinegar. Season well.

For the sauce, heat the oil in a pan and gently fry the onion and garlic for 5–8 minutes until well softened. Sprinkle over the flour and stir to

make a roux. Cook for 1 minute, stirring, then add the tomatoes. Bring to the boil, add the bay leaf and simmer for 30 minutes. Leave to cool slightly, then add the remaining ingredients and season well.

Preheat the oven to Gas Mark 4, 350°F (180°C). For the canneloni, roll out the pasta very thinly and cut into 4 × 6 inch (10 × 15cm) rectangles. Place 1–2 tablespoons filling on each rectangle, then roll up and moisten the edges with water to seal. Lay the canneloni in a large shallow greased ovenproof dish and cover with the sauce. Bake for 25–30 minutes or until the pasta is tender. Sprinkle with sunflower seeds and serve.

MUSHROOM AND RICOTTA RAVIOLI

Serve sprinkled with Parmesan cheese, or with a sauce, either tomato or Nut and Wine Sauce (page 77).

SERVES 4–6
1 tablespoon olive oil
1 onion, peeled and finely chopped
1 clove garlic, crushed
8oz (225g) button mushrooms, wiped and diced
1oz (25g) pine kernels, crushed
2 tablespoons white wine
4oz (110g) ricotta or curd cheese and crème fraîche
2 tablespoons chopped fresh basil
1 egg, beaten
salt and pepper
1 quantity Fresh Wholewheat Pasta (page 80)

Heat the oil in a pan and gently fry the onion and garlic for 4–5 minutes until softened but not coloured. Add the mushrooms and pine kernels and cook gently for 5 minutes until softened. Stir in the white wine, then increase the heat to reduce the liquid. Remove the pan from the heat, cool slightly then add the ricotta, basil and egg. Season to taste.

Roll out the pasta dough as thinly as possible and mark into 1 inch (2.5cm) squares. Place a teaspoon of filling on half the squares. Moisten the pasta in between the filling with water. Fold the remaining dough over the top and press down firmly. Cut out the squares. Leave to dry for 30 minutes.

Bring a large pan of water to the boil and add a little salt and oil. Add the ravioli and simmer for 5–6 minutes or until al dente.

RICE & GRAINS

Brown rice and other unrefined grains, principally wheat, barley, buckwheat and millet, are important staple ingredients in a wholefood vegetarian diet. From a nutritional point of view, they add fibre, protein, vitamins and minerals, and from a culinary standpoint they can be used in a variety of savoury dishes, either as an integral part such as the Wild Rice Pilaf or Persian Rice and Millet Ring or as an accompaniment, particularly to most casseroles, stews and curries. In this chapter I have suggested some simple ways of making grain side dishes more interesting.

Grains are really worth getting to know as, unlike most pulses, they need little or no preparation, merely enough time to cook. Apart from savoury dishes, you can use whole grains for puddings, salads and breakfast ideas – try the Wheatberry Cream on page 196. Buy whole grains from a health food or wholefood shop and store them in a cool dry place. They will keep at least 6 months.

Cooking rice and whole grains
Allow 2–3oz (50–75g) per person as a main course serving. I find it is easiest to measure the amount into a cup and work out the volume of water needed from there. A large cup will hold 8oz (225g) so it is a convenient way of serving 4 people:

↙ 1 cup rice needs 2 cups water
↙ 1 cup buckwheat or millet needs 3 cups water
↙ 1 cup wheat or barley needs 4 cups water

Bring the required amount of water to the boil. Add the grain, stir once and bring back to the boil. Cover and simmer until the grain is softened and cooked through. It is best if all the water is absorbed otherwise valuable vitamins and minerals will be lost when the grain is strained. Rice takes 20–30 minutes depending on the variety – short grain is quicker to cook than long grain. Use the short grain rice for risottos, stuffings and burgers as it tends to be a little stickier; use long grain rice for accompanying dishes and salads. My favourite brown rice comes from Thailand.

Wheat and barley take 50–60 minutes to cook. Use any left-over water as stock. Millet takes 18–20 minutes and buckwheat 10–15 minutes.

Opposite: Persian Rice and Millet Ring with Kumquat and Apricot Sauce (page 94)
Overleaf: Wild Rice Pilaf (page 92); Oriental Mushrooms and Cashews (page 119); Cumin Pancakes (page 107) with yoghurt raita; and Fragrant Vegetable Curry (page 122)

Grains that are fried in a little oil before cooking will have a slightly nuttier flavour. Stir them while they toast to brown as evenly as possible, but don't be concerned if one side seems darker. Pour on the correct amount of boiling water and cook as above.

When cooking grains with other vegetables, particularly juicy ones such as tomatoes, mushrooms or courgettes, you may need to adjust the liquid content; begin by using less, then add more during the cooking.

Once cooked, grains can be left to cool, and frozen, they will keep for several months.

Defrosted grains, or cold grains that have been stored in the refrigerator overnight, can be easily reheated. Heat the grain for 15 minutes in a steamer. To reheat in the oven, place the grain in a lightly greased ovenproof dish with a close fitting lid. Add a little oil or water to the grain and cover with greased greaseproof paper. Heat for 20–30 minutes at Gas Mark 4, 350°F (180°C). For a very quick alternative use a microwave oven; 2–4 minutes depending on the amount of grain.

Flours, meals and flakes
Wheat flour is the most well known and is used widely in savoury pastry or pancakes. Flours from buckwheat, rice and maize are often substituted for part of the wheat flour given in a recipe, but as they are low in gluten they do not hold together in quite the same way as wheat. Rice flour makes an excellent thickener for sauces, being lighter and more creamy than wholewheat. Maize flour, also sold as cornmeal, can be used for corn breads and Polenta (page 99), an Italian dish rather like a very thick porridge.

Oats are the most common flakes available. They are very creamy and can be quite sticky when cooked. Other flakes such as wheat, barley, rye or millet can be used as an alternative to oats. They will add a different texture and flavour.

Flakes, flours and meals do not keep as long as whole grains. Aim to use them within 2–3 months. Store in a cool dry place.

One other cereal by-product needs a mention – bulgar wheat. It is a partially cooked, cracked grain that is extremely quick to cook. For 1 cup bulgar wheat use 2–3 cups water and cook for 3–5 minutes. For a salad, soak the bulgar wheat in double the volume of boiling water until soft, then leave to cool before using. Add unsoaked bulgar wheat to soups or casseroles about 15–20 minutes before the end of cooking; it will swell up in the liquid and create an interesting texture.

Opposite: Mexican Platter (page 109)

SAVOURY BUCKWHEAT

Try different cooking liquids to add flavour to buckwheat; here mushroom stock provides a good colour and robust taste.

SERVES 4
5 dried shitake mushrooms
1 pint (570ml) boiling water
1 teaspoon sunflower oil
7oz (200g) buckwheat
1 teaspoon paprika

Soak the dried mushrooms in the water for 1–2 hours, or longer if possible. Drain, reserving the soaking liquid, and finely dice the mushrooms. Make up the reserved liquid to 1 pint (570ml).

Heat the oil in a pan and quickly sauté the buckwheat over a high heat for 2–3 minutes, stirring constantly so that the grains do not stick. Add the mushrooms, stock and paprika. Bring to the boil, cover and simmer for 15 minutes, adding more liquid if necessary. If the grain is not quite soft, cover and leave to stand for a few minutes.

WHEAT WITH CELERY AND SUNFLOWER SEEDS

Photograph on page 156
Lightly cooked sunflower seeds blend in well with the cooked grain, adding an extra nutty flavour.

SERVES 4
7oz (200g) wheatberries or whole wheatgrain
1oz (25g) sunflower seeds
2 sticks of celery, trimmed and finely diced
½ teaspoon celery seeds
2 teaspoons shoyu

Measure the wheat in a measuring jug. Place in a large pan and add four times its volume of water. Cover and simmer for 50 minutes. Check occasionally on the liquid level, adding more hot water if necessary.

Add the sunflower seeds, celery and celery seeds and cook for 5–10 minutes until the celery is just tender and the wheat is cooked. Drain and toss in the shoyu. Serve hot or cold.

BULGAR WHEAT PILAF

Bulgar wheat is the nearest you will come to a wholefood fast-food ingredient. As it is partially cooked in the processing, it is ready in minutes. Be careful not to overcook bulgar wheat or the texture can become too soft, reminiscent of baby food. In this recipe, I have chosen colourful peppers and aromatic spices to give the finished dish an attractive appearance and good flavour. You can use many other vegetables, particularly courgettes, carrots, celery, mushrooms or artichoke hearts. Puréed tomatoes make a good alternative to basic vegetable stock. As this dish is so quick to make, it is a good idea to serve it with a sauce that is virtually instantaneous too. Spiced Yoghurt (page 92) works particularly well as it is creamy in texture but has a slight tang. Serve with Toasted Nut Burgers (page 63), Tyropitas (page 151) or La Kama (page 117).

SERVES 4

1 tablespoon olive oil
1 onion, peeled and finely chopped
2 cloves garlic, crushed
1 teaspoon ground cumin
1 teaspoon ground coriander
1 teaspoon dried thyme
1 green pepper, deseeded and finely chopped
1 yellow pepper, deseeded and finely chopped
6oz (175g) bulgar wheat
2 teaspoons green peppercorns
12fl oz (350ml) boiling vegetable stock

Heat the oil in a pan and very gently fry the onion and garlic for 7–10 minutes. Add the spices and thyme and cook for a further 2–3 minutes. Stir in the peppers, cover and sweat for 5 minutes.

Add the bulgar wheat and peppercorns, stir in well and cook for a further 2 minutes. Pour over the boiling stock and cook for 10 minutes or until the liquid has been absorbed and the grain is soft.

SPICED YOGHURT

This yoghurt sauce goes very well with a pilaf (see page 91).

SERVES 4

1 tablespoon sesame seeds
1 tablespoon cumin seeds
½ pint (275ml) natural yoghurt
3fl oz (75ml) orange juice
1 clove garlic, crushed

Roast the seeds in a dry frying pan for 2–3 minutes. Crush lightly in a pestle and mortar. Mix the crushed seeds into the yoghurt with the orange juice and garlic. Leave for at least 30 minutes before serving.

WILD RICE PILAF

Photograph on page 86

Wild rice is extremely expensive. The grains are very distinctive – long, thin and almost black – and their flavour is quite mild and reminiscent of the sea. This is hardly surprising, as wild rice grows in marshy conditions. This recipe is delicious hot or cold. Serve it with Carrot and Courgette Bake (page 130) or Soufflé Spinach Pancakes (page 111).

SERVES 4

2oz (50g) sultanas
4 tablespoons orange juice
2oz (50g) wild rice
½ pint (275ml) boiling water
2oz (50g) long grain brown rice
4oz (110g) black olives, finely chopped
2 tablespoons chopped fresh parsley
1 tablespoon dry sherry
salt and pepper

Soak the sultanas in the orange juice for up to 1 hour. Meanwhile, place the wild rice in a pan with the boiling water. Cover and cook for 20 minutes. Add the brown rice and cook for a further 20 minutes or until both grains are tender. Drain the rice if necessary. Mix in the sultanas, olives, parsley and sherry. Season to taste and serve hot or cold.

SPICED MILLET

This dish is mildly spiced and golden in colour.

SERVES 4
2 tablespoons sunflower oil
2 onions, peeled and finely chopped
2 teaspoons ground cinnamon
1 teaspoon ground turmeric
1 teaspoon ground cardamom
pinch of curry powder
8oz (225g) millet grain
1–2 tablespoons lemon juice
salt and pepper

Heat the oil in a pan and very slowly cook the onions for 10–15 minutes until well softened but not coloured. Mix the spices with a little water. Add to the onions and fry for 3–4 minutes.

Measure the millet in a measuring jug, then add to the spice mixture and cook for 2–3 minutes, stirring well.

Measure boiling water to three times the volume of millet, and pour over the millet. Bring back to the boil, stir once, cover and simmer for 18–20 minutes. Check on the water level occasionally, adding more if necessary. If the grain is not quite cooked, leave to stand, covered, for a few minutes. Season with lemon juice, salt and pepper. Serve hot or cold.

FRUITY BARLEY

This is a light, herby grain dish with the refreshing tang of lemon.

SERVES 4
1 teaspoon sunflower oil
8oz (225g) barley, rinsed and drained
2 tablespoons concentrated apple juice
2 tablespoons sunflower oil
juice of 1/2 lemon
1 tablespoon tarragon vinegar
2 tablespoons finely chopped fresh parsley
2 teaspoons chopped fresh tarragon
salt

Heat the 1 teaspoon oil in a pan and lightly fry the barley for 2–3 minutes, stirring well. Pour over 2 pints (1.1 litres) boiling water and cook for 50–60 minutes. Alternatively, pressure cook for 20 minutes. Drain if necessary when cooked.

Mix the apple juice, 2 tablespoons sunflower oil, lemon juice and vinegar together and pour over the freshly cooked barley. Leave to cool. Toss in the fresh herbs and add salt to taste.

To serve hot, leave out the herbs, add extra oil to the barley and transfer to an ovenproof dish and cover. Bake for 10–15 minutes at Gas Mark 4, 350°F (180°C) or microwave on full power for 3 minutes. Add the fresh herbs and salt before serving.

PERSIAN RICE AND MILLET RING WITH KUMQUAT AND APRICOT SAUCE

Photograph on page 85

Serving cooked grains in a moulded shape such as a pudding basin or, better still, a savarin ring, means you can put contrasting sauces and vegetables in the centre. Short grain rice and millet are ideal as they can both be quite sticky once cooked and will hold their shape. If you prefer peeled broad beans, blanch them first and the beans will pop out easily. This dish requires a moist accompaniment, so I have suggested a tangy kumquat sauce which is easy to make. This ring can easily be transformed into a splendid salad. Add Herb Vinaigrette (page 177) to both the beans and grains, and chill the sauce thoroughly. Save some of the fresh herbs to use as a garnish. Serve with green vegetables such as courgettes, stir-fried spinach or Artichoke and Asparagus Salad (page 178).

SERVES 4
1 tablespoon olive oil
9oz (250g) mixed short grain rice and millet
1¼ pints (700ml) boiling water
salt and pepper
1 onion, peeled and finely sliced
1 clove garlic, crushed
8oz (225g) broad beans
2 tablespoons chopped fresh coriander
2 tablespoons chopped fresh mint
1 teaspoon ground allspice

Sauce
8oz (225g) kumquats, quartered
2oz (50g) dried apricots, cut in slivers
½ pint (275ml) water
½–1oz (15–25g) sugar
Garnish
fresh mint leaves

Brush the pan with a little of the oil and lightly roast the rice and millet for 2–3 minutes, stirring well. Pour on the boiling water, bring back to the boil, stir once or twice, then cover and simmer for 20–25 minutes or until the rice is tender and the liquid is absorbed. Stir once or twice during cooking and do not worry if the millet overcooks slightly, as this will help the grains stick together. Season the cooked grains well.

Pack the grain mixture in a lightly greased deep 8–9 inch (20–23cm) savarin ring, cover with greased greaseproof paper and keep warm in the oven.

Heat the oil in a pan and lightly fry the onion for 5–6 minutes until just softened. Add the garlic and cook for 1 minute. Add the broad beans and stir fry for 3–4 minutes, adding a little water if you prefer them soft. Toss in the coriander, mint and allspice. Season to taste.

For the sauce, mix the kumquats with the apricots in a pan and cover with the water. Simmer gently for 30 minutes or until the fruit is soft and the liquid reduced. Add sugar to taste and cook for another 10 minutes.

Turn out the mould, fill the centre with the broad bean mixture and surround with kumquat sauce. Serve hot, garnished with mint leaves.

RICE WITH ORANGE
AND RAISIN KORMA

Tamarind and roasted seeds form the basis of this aromatic recipe in which the onions are cooked then braised in the spices. Adding yoghurt can be tricky as it is likely to separate when heated. One solution is to mix in some gram flour or cornflour. Alternatively, add only a couple of tablespoons at a time, stirring constantly so that all the moisture evaporates and the mixture is heated right through. The resulting sauce should be rich and thick. Serve this korma with a bean dish or bean purée, or a well flavoured salad including some raw onion.

SERVES 4

1 pint (570ml) water
8oz (225g) long grain brown rice
Sauce
2oz (50g) dry tamarind
1 teaspoon cumin seeds
½ teaspoon fenugreek seeds
1 tablespoon sunflower oil
8oz (225g) onions, peeled and finely chopped
1 large red pepper, deseeded and diced
2 cloves garlic, crushed
½ teaspoon ground turmeric
½ teaspoon chilli powder
1 tablespoon grated fresh ginger root
1 teaspoon garam masala
8fl oz (225ml) natural full-fat yoghurt
3oz (75g) raisins
2 tablespoons orange juice
salt and pepper

Bring the water to the boil in a pan, add the rice, stir once and bring back to boiling point. Cover and simmer for 25–30 minutes or until the rice is tender and the water absorbed.

For the sauce, steep the tamarind in just enough hot water to cover for about 30 minutes. Mash gently, removing any seeds or stones, to make a thick pulp.

Toast the seeds under a grill or in a dry frying pan for 1–2 minutes. Grind in a pestle and mortar.

Heat the oil in a pan and gently fry the onions for 10 minutes until soft but not coloured. Add the red pepper and cook for 4–5 minutes.

Mix the ground seeds with the garlic, the remaining spices and tamarind pulp. Add to the onion mixture and cook for 10 minutes. Add 2 tablespoons of the yoghurt and cook, stirring, until the liquid has evaporated. Keep adding 2 tablespoons at a time until all the yoghurt is used up. Stir in the raisins and orange juice, mixing well. Season to taste. Serve the rice hot, topped with the sauce.

RICH MUSHROOM RISOTTO

It is certainly worth buying these dried Italian mushrooms as they provide a wonderful full-bodied flavour. Unfortunately, porcini are expensive but you do not need many and the remainder will keep more or less indefinitely. Dried mushrooms on their own would be overpowering, so balance out the taste by using some fresh mushrooms. I prefer to cook these separately so that the texture is distinct and their flavour is not diminished. You could serve Summer Vegetable Cocktail (page 42) or Sunflower Soufflés (page 61) as a starter, and accompany the risotto with a simple green vegetable or salad.

SERVES 4

2oz (50g) dried Italian mushrooms (porcini)
1 pint (570ml) boiling water
3 tablespoons olive oil
1 large onion, peeled and finely chopped
2 cloves garlic, crushed
8oz (225g) carrots, peeled and diced
8–10oz (225–275g) short grain rice
2 tablespoons red wine
8oz (225g) button mushrooms, wiped and halved
1 clove garlic
2 tablespoons chopped fresh parsley
salt and pepper

Soak the dried mushrooms in the boiling water for 1–2 hours. Drain well, reserving the stock.

Heat 2 tablespoons of the oil in a pan and gently fry the onion for 8–10 minutes until soft but not coloured. Add the garlic and fry for 2 minutes. Stir in the carrots and cook for 3–4 minutes. Add the rice and cook for 2 minutes. Pour over the reserved mushroom stock, stir and bring to the boil. Cover and simmer for 20–25 minutes or until the rice is cooked and the stock absorbed. Check on the liquid level once or twice during cooking, adding more water if necessary. Stir in the wine during the last 5 minutes.

In a separate pan, heat the remaining oil and lightly fry the button mushrooms for a few minutes. Add the garlic, parsley and soaked dried mushrooms and cook for 5–6 minutes, stirring frequently, until the mushrooms are well softened. Be careful that the dried mushrooms do not stick. Toss the cooked mushrooms into the freshly cooked rice. Season to taste and serve straight away.

BAKED GNOCCHI

There are many varieties of gnocchi in Italy; either potatoes, semolina or breadcrumbs are used as base, and the mixture is enriched with cheese or eggs and flavoured with basil, spinach or other Italian herbs. Many of these staple peasant dishes were originally designed to use everyday ingredients, making cheap but filling meals. The sauces served with gnocchi add most of the interest and flavour. The simplest idea is to toss the gnocchi in a little butter or flavoured oil, then add grated Parmesan cheese. You could certainly serve it that way as a starter. When making gnocchi it can be tricky to obtain the right consistency so that it does not break up when boiled, or become too solid. My recipe is for a baked version which keeps the mixture light and cake-like. You could also use gnocchi with a fruit sauce as a sweet dish. For a plainer sweet version, fry in butter and dust with sugar and ground cinnamon.

SERVES 4-6
½ pint (275ml) skimmed milk
5oz (150g) wholewheat semolina
3oz (75g) ricotta cheese
2 eggs, beaten
salt and pepper
butter and olive oil for frying

Preheat the oven to Gas Mark 4, 350°F (180°C). Heat the milk gently in a pan, then stir in the semolina. Bring to the boil, stirring, until thickened. Simmer for 4 minutes, stirring constantly, until very thick. Remove the pan from the heat, cool slightly, then beat in the ricotta cheese and eggs. Season very well.

Spoon the mixture into a Swiss roll tin lined with greaseproof paper. Bake for 20 minutes. Turn out of the tin and leave to cool. Mark into small squares.

Melt a little butter and olive oil and fry the gnocchi squares for 2–3 minutes until crispy and well heated through. Serve hot with Cream Cheese Sauce (opposite) or Cheese and Chilli Sauce (page 100), grated Parmesan cheese, tomato sauce or vegetable ratatouille.

CREAM CHEESE SAUCE

To serve gnocchi (opposite) as a main course, accompany with a substantial sauce such as this rich and luxurious recipe. You could serve a plain steamed green vegetable or a casserole with it.

SERVES 4

1oz (25g) butter
6oz (175g) strong-flavoured Cheddar cheese or blue cheese, grated or crumbled
¼ pint (150ml) single cream or full-fat milk
2 teaspoons white wine vinegar
2 teaspoons finely chopped fresh sage
salt and pepper

Gently melt the butter in a small pan and stir in the cheese. Allow the cheese to melt slowly over a low heat. Remove the pan from the heat, whisk in the cream and vinegar and stir in the sage. Return the pan to the heat and cook, stirring, until the sauce is quite hot and the sage turns a brilliant green. Season to taste. Serve immediately with gnocchi or pasta.

POLENTA

This classic dish from northern Italy is soft and light inside and has a crisp outer coating when fried. Traditionally polenta is deep fried, but shallow frying is fine as long as the pieces are browned evenly. Serve polenta with Cheese and Chilli Sauce (page 100), a classic tomato sauce, or try Marinated Vegetable Sauce (page 75). Polenta can be served as an accompaniment to a vegetable dish such as Baked Pumpkin with Leeks and Cream (page 169) or with any of the sauces from the pasta chapter.

SERVES 4

2 pints (1.1 litres) water
8oz (225g) cornmeal
1 teaspoon salt
2oz (50g) sunflower margarine or butter
sunflower oil for shallow frying
Coating
1 egg, beaten
1–2 tablespoons cornmeal

Bring the water to the boil in a large pan. Sprinkle over the cornmeal and beat in well to prevent any lumps forming. Stir in the salt and margarine. Reduce the heat to very low, cover and cook for 20 minutes, stirring frequently, until it has a creamy, thick consistency. You may find it safer to cook polenta in a double boiler as there is less chance of it sticking.

Spoon the mixture into a lightly greased 13 × 9 inch (33 × 23cm) dish and leave to cool. When cold, cut the polenta into small squares. Dip each one first into beaten egg and then the cornmeal. Shallow fry for 3 minutes until crisp and golden, turning the pieces over frequently. Serve warm with Cheese and Chilli Sauce (below).

CHEESE AND CHILLI SAUCE

This is a spicy cheese and tomato sauce with Mexican overtones. Polenta (page 99) has quite a mild flavour, so whatever sauce you choose, make sure it has a strong taste and a good colour that contrasts with the golden cornmeal. You could also use this sauce with traditional Mexican tortillas (page 108).

SERVES 4

1 tablespoon olive oil
1 onion, peeled and finely chopped
1 clove garlic, crushed
6 large tomatoes, skinned and chopped
generous pinch of chilli powder
1 red pepper, deseeded and diced
4oz (110g) cheese, grated
salt and pepper

Heat the oil in a medium pan and gently fry the onion and garlic for 4–5 minutes until soft but not coloured. Add the tomatoes, chilli and red pepper and cook for 10–15 minutes until the tomatoes have softened.

Remove the pan from the heat and stir in 3oz (75g) of the grated cheese. Stir until the cheese melts, then season to taste. Serve with polenta and sprinkle the remaining cheese on top.

PANCAKES

Delicious and adaptable, pancakes are little trouble to make. Many people tend to think of them as being sweet, or related to a once-a-year appearance on Shrove Tuesday. However, they are an extremely easy way to present a meal and, by using wholewheat flour as suggested in the basic batter recipe, they are very nutritious as well. I also give advice in this chapter on using other flours for batters, preparing the pancakes in advance, freezing and reheating.

There are traditional batter-style dishes made in many other cuisines, such as the Mexican tortilla, Russian blini and Indian pancake. Apart from the fillings suggested, use filling recipes from the vegetable chapter such as Steamed Courgettes (page 164) or Creamed Celeriac (page 162) and also small quantities of casseroles, particularly Oriental Mushrooms and Cashews (page 119), or a curry such as the Fragrant Vegetable Curry (page 122) or Tandoori Tofu and Potato Curry (page 124).

As pancakes are such an easy way to entertain, not only because of presentation but also because so much can be prepared in advance, I have included two spectacular and sumptuous dishes at the end of the chapter – a layered galette with contrasting vegetable layers, and Soufflé Spinach Pancakes.

BASIC PANCAKES

Making wholewheat pancakes is not difficult, especially with appliances such as a food processor or blender to make the batter smooth and light. It is also worth investing in a good quality small non-stick frying pan as that will yield perfect results nearly every time. Wholewheat batter is more substantial than a white flour batter, so be prepared to add a little more liquid if necessary. It is a good idea to let the batter stand for a while before using to give it a chance to thicken, then you can easily see if it needs diluting. A non-dairy batter can be made with soya milk, enriched with a tablespoon of soya flour with a little baking powder added to make it lighter. Handle this batter more carefully as it lacks the egg's binding quality. Richer batters can be made with more eggs and skim-med milk powder.

Replace some of the wholewheat flour with buckwheat flour or maize flour for a change. The former will yield a dark speckled batter char-

acterised by the tang of buckwheat; the latter, a light golden mixture. Versions of pancakes can be made solely with these flours but as they are both lacking in gluten, the elastic protein that helps hold the batter together, be prepared for the end results to be more fragile.

Apart from a good pan, the only other ingredients for success with pancakes are time and organisation. Have on hand a little oil and a brush to grease the pan in between making each pancake and have the batter ready in a jug as it is easier to pour than from a blender goblet or food processor.

MAKES 8–10 PANCAKES

½ pint (275ml) milk, skimmed or whole
1 egg
1 teaspoon sunflower oil
4oz (110g) wholewheat flour
pinch of salt

Blend the milk, egg and oil together in a blender or food processor until smooth. Add the flour and salt and blend again. If possible leave the mixture to stand for about 30 minutes. Blend again and adjust the liquid content if necessary.

Heat a small non-stick frying pan and brush with a little oil. Fry 2 tablespoons of batter at a time, tilting it round the pan so the batter spreads out evenly. Reduce the heat slightly and cook the pancake for 1–2 minutes on each side.

Once cooked, if you intend to eat them straight away, pile the pancakes onto a warm plate and keep them in a low oven or over a pan of simmering water.

If you are preparing pancakes ahead of time, leave them to cool completely before stacking and wrapping in greaseproof paper or foil. Pancakes will keep 3–4 days in the refrigerator. Alternatively, freeze them for up to 4 months. Filled and frozen, pancakes will keep for up to 2 months. To defrost, unwrap and leave for about 20 minutes. Reheat in a lightly greased pan for about 30 seconds each side.

Filled pancakes can be baked from frozen. Cover first with a sauce, foil or greased greaseproof paper and heat in the oven at Gas Mark 6, 400°F (200°C) for 25–30 minutes. Remember, filled pancakes can be rolled plainly or cornet style, folded in envelopes or layered in a galette.

CRÊPES FORESTIÈRE

These traditional savoury crêpes from France can be made with a whole-wheat flour or a mixture of wholewheat and buckwheat flours and filled with a rich sauce of peas, nuts, cream and parsley. Once rolled up, the pancakes are covered with sauce and topped with cheese, then baked. It is easy to prepare this type of dish in advance for a special occasion. Simply reheat for serving and add a fresh garnish. The pale green filling is enhanced by serving side vegetables such as a dark green spinach purée and Hot Beetroot with Spicy Apple Sauce (page 161).

SERVES 4
½ pint (275ml) skimmed milk
1 egg
1 teaspoon olive oil
4oz (110g) wholewheat flour or 2oz (50g) each of wholewheat and buckwheat flours
generous pinch of salt
Filling
1lb (450g) peas
1½oz (40g) butter or margarine
2oz (50g) shallots, peeled and finely chopped
1 clove garlic, crushed
1½oz (40g) brown rice flour
1 pint (570ml) skimmed milk
1 bay leaf
2 teaspoons chopped fresh tarragon
3 tablespoons finely chopped fresh parsley
1oz (25g) walnuts, ground
salt and pepper
2 tablespoons single cream
4oz (110g) strong-flavoured cheese

For the crêpes, beat the milk with the egg and oil in a food processor or blender. Add the flour and salt and beat until smooth. Leave the batter to stand for up to 1 hour then beat again if necessary. Using a small frying pan, cook 8 crêpes one at a time, using 2 tablespoons batter, and set aside.

Preheat the oven to Gas Mark 4, 350°F (180°C). For the filling, place the peas in a pan of boiling salted water and simmer gently for 5–6 minutes until just tender. Drain and leave to cool. Gently melt the butter in a small pan and cook the shallots for 5 minutes until softened, then add the garlic and cook for 1 minute. Sprinkle over the brown rice flour and

stir in to make a roux. Gradually add the milk, about a third at a time, and stir well until smooth. Bring to the boil, add the bay leaf, tarragon and parsley, then simmer for 3–4 minutes, stirring occasionally. Mix in the ground walnuts and season well. Pour half the sauce over the cooked peas, add the cream and stir in well so that the peas are well coated.

Fill each crêpe with 1–2 tablespoons of the pea filling. Roll up and place in a large oiled ovenproof dish. Any remaining filling can be placed at the sides. Cover the crêpes with the remaining sauce and sprinkle with grated cheese. Heat through in the oven for about 10–15 minutes until the cheese is melted and the sauce just bubbling. Serve hot.

CHEESE AND OLIVE FILLING

This is a particularly robust pancake filling with the strong flavour of feta cheese and olives. It is essential to make a thick vegetable filling for pancakes – here a tomato coulis is used to moisten the mixture – otherwise the end result will be disappointing. This filling mixture can be made in advance as it improves on standing. Serve with buckwheat or wholewheat pancakes, or with tortillas (page 108) for a different type of meal. A leafy salad or creamy bean pâté would make a good starter.

FILLS 6–8 PANCAKES
1 tablespoon olive oil
1 onion, peeled and finely chopped
2 cloves garlic, crushed
2 sticks of celery, diced
1 tablespoon dried oregano
2oz (50g) black olives, sliced
1 × 14oz (400g) tin of tomatoes, well drained
1 tablespoon tomato purée
6oz (175g) feta cheese, cubed
3 tablespoons finely chopped fresh parsley
salt and pepper

Heat the oil in a pan and cook the onion for 5–7 minutes. Add the garlic and celery and cook for 10 minutes until very well softened. Stir in the oregano, olives, tomatoes and tomato purée and cook for 25–30 minutes, stirring occasionally, until reduced to a thick, rich sauce. Add the cheese and parsley and mix in well. Season to taste. Use to fill pancakes of your choice.

WHOLEWHEAT BLINIS

This batter is unusual as fresh yeast is used as a raising agent and an egg white is folded into the mixture to create a soufflé effect. The pancakes, the size of drop scones, are then fried briefly on both sides, leaving the centre light and fluffy. A mixture of buckwheat and wholewheat flours gives the batter a dark speckled appearance and strong flavour. Blinis need to be cooked and eaten straight away. This quantity makes enough for a main course, but you could halve the amounts to make an unusual starter for a meal. Accompany with a well flavoured or tangy sauce. Natural yoghurt, soured cream or smetana all work well, and their creamy colours are a good contrast. Alternatives to dairy products are moist vegetable sauces, particularly those with sweet and sour flavours and a chutney-like consistency.

SERVES 3–4 AS A MAIN COURSE OR 6 AS A STARTER

½oz (15g) fresh yeast
½ teaspoon brown sugar
8fl oz (225ml) warm water
2 eggs, separated
4oz (110g) wholewheat flour
4oz (110g) buckwheat flour
pinch of salt
butter for frying

For the batter, mix the yeast and sugar together in a bowl, then pour in the water and stir well. Leave to rest in a warm place for 5 minutes, then beat in the egg yolks. Sift the flours and salt together and beat into the yeast mixture until smooth. The resulting batter should be as thick as double cream; add a little more warm water if necessary. Cover and leave in a warm place for about 1 hour, then beat the batter again.

Whisk the egg whites until stiff. Stir 2 tablespoons of the egg white into the batter, then carefully fold in the remaining egg white, keeping in as much air as possible. Leave the batter to rest for 20 minutes.

Melt the butter in a heavy frying pan and, using a tablespoon of batter for each blini, fry 2–3 at a time for 2–3 minutes on each side. Keep the cooked blinis warm while you prepare the remainder.

Serve the blinis simply with natural yoghurt, smetana or soured cream. Alternatively, serve with Cottage Cheese Dressing (page 179).

CUMIN PANCAKES WITH FRESH TOMATO AND SULTANA RELISH

Photograph on page 87

This recipe is for small, thick Indian pancakes. Serve hot or cold like a bread with a casserole, curry or soup, or as a first course.

MAKES 6–8
1 teaspoon cumin seeds
2oz (50g) rice flour
2oz (50g) wholewheat semolina
pinch of salt
¼ pint (150ml) natural yoghurt
2–3fl oz (50–75ml) water
sunflower oil for shallow frying
Relish
1½lb (700g) Italian tomatoes, wiped
1 tablespoon sunflower oil
1 onion, peeled and finely chopped
2 cloves garlic, crushed
2oz (50g) sultanas
1 tablespoon tomato purée
1 tablespoon concentrated apple juice
1 teaspoon grated fresh root ginger
pinch of cayenne
salt and pepper

Preheat the oven to Gas Mark 4, 350°F (180°C). For the relish, bake the tomatoes in an ovenproof dish for 30 minutes or until soft. Skin, then purée in a blender or food processor and sieve to remove the seeds.

Heat the oil in a pan and gently fry the onion for 3–4 minutes until just softened. Add the garlic and cook for 1 minute. Stir in the tomato pulp, sultanas, tomato purée, concentrated apple juice, ginger and cayenne. Stir well and simmer, uncovered, for 30–40 minutes or until the mixture is reduced to a thick consistency. Season and serve at room temperature.

For the pancakes, roast the cumin seeds lightly in a dry frying pan for 2–3 minutes until they release their aroma. Mix the rice flour, semolina and salt together in a bowl. Add the yoghurt and water and mix well to form a smooth thick batter. Stir in the cumin seeds. Brush a small pan with a little oil and heat thoroughly. Make the pancakes the size of small saucers, cooking for about 1 minute on each side. Pile onto a warmed plate and keep warm. Serve the pancakes with the relish, raita or other dishes.

TORTILLAS WITH CHEESE AND SWEETCORN SAUCE

Tortillas are traditional Mexican pancakes made from maize or corn-meal. They are fried on a hot griddle or in a heavy saucepan until lightly browned, giving them their familiar mottled effect. When warm, they are very pliable and can be filled and folded in half. If you do not want to fill them straight away, leave to cool on a plate, then reheat the tortillas in a warm oven until soft enough to fold and fill, either with this Cheese and Sweetcorn Sauce or another filling from this chapter.

SERVES 4–6
12fl oz (350ml) water
1½oz (40g) sunflower margarine
5oz (150g) cornmeal
5oz (150g) wholewheat flour
pinch of salt
2 tablespoons olive paste or finely minced olives
Sauce
3 tablespoons olive oil
1 large onion, peeled and finely chopped
1 green chilli, deseeded and finely diced
1½oz (40g) wholewheat flour
1 pint (570ml) skimmed milk
4oz (110g) Cheddar cheese, grated
12oz (350g) sweetcorn kernels
1 red pepper, deseeded and diced
salt and pepper
extra grated cheese for serving

For the tortillas, bring the water to the boil in a medium, preferably non-stick, pan and add ¾oz (20g) of the margarine. Stir in the corn-meal, cover and cook over a very low heat for 5 minutes. Stir in the remaining margarine until smooth, remove pan from the heat and leave to cool.

Mix the flour and salt together in a large bowl and stir in the cooked cornmeal. Knead the mixture to a soft dough, adding a little more water or flour to obtain the right consistency. Beat in the olive paste or minced olives. Divide the dough into twelve equal sized pieces. Roll out each one into a 6–7 inch (15–18cm) round.

To cook the tortillas, heat a heavy frying pan well. Cook the tortillas

for 2–3 minutes on each side until flecked with dark spots. Immediately fold them gently in half so they retain this shape as they cool. Alternatively, cool the tortillas flat, then reheat and fold just before serving.

For the sauce, heat the oil in a pan and gently fry the onion for 7–10 minutes until soft but not coloured. Add the chilli and cook for 2 minutes. Sprinkle over the flour, stir until smooth and cook for 1–2 minutes. Gradually add the milk a third at a time, stirring continuously. Bring to the boil and simmer for 3–4 minutes, stirring frequently.

Mix together half the grated cheese, the sweetcorn and red pepper in a bowl. Pour over a third of the sauce, mix in well and season to taste. Fold the remaining cheese into the white sauce.

To serve, fill each tortilla with a little cheese and sweetcorn sauce and place in a flameproof serving dish. Coat with the remaining cheese sauce, sprinkle with extra cheese and grill until golden brown. Serve hot.

MEXICAN PLATTER

Photograph on page 88

As an alternative to eating tortillas hot and filled as a main course, leave until cold, then tear them into small pieces and use for dipping into sauces and relishes or eating with crudités, crunchy vegetables or mixed salads. For a Mexican theme, serve cherry tomatoes, spring onions, diced hard cheese, sliced peppers and black olives with the guacamole given here or the Avocado and Apple Dip on page 50.

SERVES 4–6
12 tortillas (above)
1 avocado
juice of ½ lemon
2 cloves garlic, crushed
pepper
1 tablespoon olive oil (optional)

Make the tortillas, then prepare a selection of accompaniments.

For the guacamole, mash the avocado with the lemon juice and garlic. Season well with pepper and add a little olive oil, if liked.

Serve on a large platter with the tortillas.

LAYERED PANCAKE GALETTE

This pancake idea is excellent for a party piece. There is a fair amount of preparation but most can be done in advance, so all you need to do at the last minute is assemble the galette and heat it through. Use either wholewheat or buckwheat pancakes as the base.

SERVES 4
1 quantity wholewheat or
buckwheat pancake batter (page 102)
Filling 1
12oz (350g) mangetout, trimmed
2 tablespoons soured cream
1oz (25g) cream cheese
3 spring onions, trimmed and diced
salt and pepper
Filling 2
1 tablespoon olive oil
8oz (225g) fennel, diced
6–8 artichoke hearts, sliced
1 × 14oz (400g) tin of tomatoes, puréed
1 tablespoon tomato purée
1 teaspoon chopped fresh tarragon
1 bay leaf
2–3 tablespoons grated Parmesan cheese for serving

Make the pancakes as on page 102 and set aside to cool.

For the first filling, steam the mangetout for 5–6 minutes. Cool slightly, then purée in a blender or food processor with the soured cream and cream cheese. Stir in the spring onions and season to taste.

For the second filling, heat the oil in a pan and gently cook the fennel for 5 minutes until beginning to soften. Add the artichoke hearts and cook for 2–3 minutes. Stir in the tomatoes, tomato purée, tarragon and bay leaf. Bring to the boil and simmer, uncovered, for 30–40 minutes until thick and pulpy.

Preheat the oven to Gas Mark 4, 350°F (180°C). Place a pancake in a loose-based 7 inch (18cm) cake tin. Spoon over a layer of mangetout filling. Cover with a second pancake and a layer of artichoke filling. Continue these layers until all the fillings and pancakes are used up.

Heat the pancakes in the oven for 15 minutes, covering the top one with foil. Turn out and sprinkle with Parmesan cheese. Serve hot, accompanied by tomato sauce.

SOUFFLÉ SPINACH PANCAKES WITH MUSHROOMS

You can add a variety of ingredients to a basic pancake batter. With spinach purée I add extra milk and an egg to lighten the mixture, and I cook the batter in small spoonfuls, rather like drop scones, as they are easier to fry and turn over. You could simply make a batch of small pancakes, arrange them on a plate and cover with sauce. For a more impressive dish, layer the pancakes with the sauce, cover with topping and bake until set. The pancakes rise during baking and blend into the sauce, creating a soufflé effect which is quite delicious. Serve with a grain dish of rice or wheat, or hot pasta tossed in oil and garlic. Fennel and Celeriac Soup (page 37) would make a good starter.

SERVES 4

1 tablespoon olive oil
1lb (450g) spinach, washed and shredded
1 clove garlic, crushed
4oz (110g) wholewheat flour
1/2 teaspoon salt
3/4 pint (450ml) skimmed milk
2 eggs
2 tablespoons chopped fresh coriander
Sauce
1 tablespoon olive oil
1 onion, peeled and finely chopped
2 cloves garlic, crushed
1/2 teaspoon ground coriander
8oz (225g) field mushrooms, wiped and thickly sliced
1/2oz (15g) sunflower margarine
1/2oz (15g) wholewheat flour
up to 1/2 pint (275ml) skimmed milk
1 tablespoon tomato purée
1 tablespoon shoyu
pepper
Topping
1/2 pint (275ml) mixed natural yoghurt and soured cream
juice of 1/2 lemon
1 egg
Garnish
2 tablespoons finely chopped fresh coriander

For the pancakes, heat the oil in a large pan and stir fry the spinach. Add the garlic, cover and leave the spinach to wilt for 2–3 minutes. Drain if necessary, then purée in a blender or food processor until smooth. Beat in the flour and salt. Whisk together the milk and eggs and blend thoroughly into the spinach mixture. Stir in the fresh coriander. The resulting batter will be fairly thick.

Using the minimum of oil in a medium frying pan, fry tablespoons of batter, about 4 at a time, turning them over after about 2 minutes. (This quantity makes 35 to 40 little pancakes.) Leave to cool.

Preheat the oven to Gas Mark 4, 350°F (180°C). For the sauce, heat the oil in a pan and gently fry the onion for 5–7 minutes. Add the garlic and ground coriander and cook for 2 minutes. Stir in the mushrooms and cook for 10 minutes, stirring frequently. Drain off the juice and reserve.

In a separate small pan, melt the margarine, sprinkle over the flour and cook for 2 minutes, stirring until smooth. Add enough milk to the mushroom juice to make ½ pint (275ml). Gradually add the liquid, stirring frequently. Bring to the boil and simmer for 2 minutes. Stir in the cooked mushrooms, tomato purée and shoyu. Season to taste.

Using a large ovenproof dish, put a layer of pancakes on the base and cover with mushroom sauce. Repeat the layers twice, finishing with sauce.

For the topping, beat the yoghurt, soured cream, lemon juice and egg together. Pour over the mushroom sauce. Bake for 25–30 minutes until the topping has set. Just before serving, sprinkle over fresh coriander.

CASSEROLES
& CURRIES

Every corner of the world has its own familiar casserole featuring its own combination of herbs and spices – not surprising as they are so simple to make and easy to vary with different vegetables. Start with 2–2½lb (1kg) vegetables to serve 4 people.

Casseroles should be moist and juicy, but not too liquid so they become soup. Add bulgar wheat or pasta to thicken the mixture, or use tofu or cooked beans, from the freezer or a tin, if the concoction of vegetables is not substantial enough. Notes on how to cook and freeze beans are on page 232. Stew-type recipes always work well with dry accompaniments such as grains, which will soak up the liquid of the dish. Couscous (produced from semolina) can be steamed in a fine sieve or couscousiere above the casserole for about 20 minutes.

Alternative accompaniments are jacket baked potatoes or hearty chunks of bread. Another idea is to make a topping for the casserole; mashed potato is a splendid choice – it is such a familiar sight that it may mean you can be a little more adventurous with what's underneath. You could also make a corn batter such as the one used on the Golden Pie on page 132, a savoury pastry, or use the crumble topping from Almond and Broccoli Gratin (page 128).

As most casseroles benefit from being made in advance or being cooked for a long time, remember that the vegetables will be fairly soft by serving time, so keep them chunky to give the dish a good visual appeal and prevent it from being a mush. Make sure there are some crisp accompaniments – crunchy, lightly steamed vegetables as a side dish, or toasted or spiced nuts such as Spiced Cashew Nuts with Chilli (page 69) scattered on at the last moment. A few raw vegetables, or cubes of fruit in the case of the Caribbean casserole, can be added.

Casseroles from around the world are included in this chapter – piquant Polish fricassée, oriental mushroom ragout, a sweet spicy idea from the Caribbean, an aromatic Middle Eastern stew and a classic Mexican dish featuring beans. The curry recipes, three from India and one from Thailand, cover a range of different spices. Eat them with some of the accompaniments I have outlined or use smaller quantities as fillings for pancakes. Although these recipes are simmered on the hob, they could be cooked in the oven at Gas Mark 4–5, 350–375°F (180–190°C); they will need less looking after but may take longer to cook.

Stews freeze well providing there is enough moisture to prevent the mixture becoming dry when reheated. A predominantly vegetable dish will tend to go mushy, so do not cook it as long initially. Highly spiced dishes do not keep as long because the flavours change, so freeze for up to 2 months only.

MEXICAN BEANS

Beans are a staple ingredient of a vegetarian diet. They are fairly cheap to buy and, once cooked, it is easy to make them into tasty casseroles by adding various combinations of ingredients. In this recipe I have used spices for flavouring as well as different coloured peppers, which not only look good but are moist and juicy and complement the floury quality of the beans. Serve with rice, barley or a baked jacket potato.

SERVES 4

8oz (225g) canellini or haricot beans, soaked overnight
2 tablespoons olive oil
2 onions, peeled and coarsely chopped
2 cloves garlic, crushed
1 teaspoon cumin seeds
½ teaspoon aniseeds
½ teaspoon ground cinnamon
pinch of chilli powder
1 red pepper, deseeded and cut into thin strips
1 yellow pepper, deseeded and cut into thin strips
1 green pepper, deseeded and cut into thin strips
2 tablespoons tomato purée
¼ pint (150ml) bean stock
⅓ pint (200ml) light beer
12 black olives, coarsely chopped
salt and pepper
Garnish
3oz (75g) Cheddar cheese, cubed
1 avocado, diced

Drain the beans and rinse well. Place in a pan, cover with plenty of fresh water and bring to the boil. Boil fiercely for 10 minutes, then cover and simmer for 35–40 minutes or until the beans are cooked. Drain, reserving the stock.

Heat the oil in a pan and gently cook the onion for 8–10 minutes until soft but not coloured. Add the garlic and spices and cook for 3 minutes. Mix in the peppers and cooked beans and cook for 10 minutes.

Dissolve the tomato purée in the reserved stock and add to the beans. Cover and cook slowly for about 40 minutes, stirring occasionally. Add the beer and olives and cook for a further 15 minutes. Season to taste. Top with the cheese and avocado just before serving.

CARIBBEAN CASSEROLE

This tasty casserole has a Caribbean influence in its use of spices, a mildly hot but sweet mixture, and also in the choice of vegetables, sweet potato and green banana. Both of these are quite similar to the ordinary white potato, giving a mealy quality once cooked. Sweet potatoes have a purplish red skin. The white firm flesh has a mild chestnut flavour, hence their sweetness. Yams, which could be used instead, are not quite as sweet. Green bananas can be found in ethnic vegetable markets and in some greengrocers. They are used for boiling and frying and have a floury texture once cooked. Do not be tempted to bite into them raw as it is a most unpleasant experience. If you cannot obtain green bananas, unripe yellow ones make a fair substitute. I like serving casseroles with an interesting range of fresh garnishes, as these provide a crisp texture in contrast to the well cooked vegetables. Bright colours enhance the appearance. In this recipe, the pineapple garnish adds a sweet yet acidic touch complementing the other ingredients. Serve with millet or rice. For a starter, try a creamy dip such as Courgette and Cheese (page 49) or Red Pepper and Sunflower (page 50), served with Sesame Bread Sticks (page 198).

SERVES 4
1 tablespoon groundnut oil
1 onion, peeled and finely chopped
1 clove garlic, crushed
½ teaspoon chopped fresh root ginger
1 teaspoon curry powder
½ teaspoon ground coriander
2 cloves
pinch of cayenne
1lb (450g) sweet potato or yam, peeled and cubed
1lb (450g) courgettes, marrow or squash, thickly sliced
2–3 green bananas, peeled and thickly sliced
¼ pint (150ml) tomato juice
juice of 1 small lime
2 tablespoons rum
little vegetable stock if necessary
salt and pepper
Garnish
4 spring onions, trimmed and finely chopped
4 slices of fresh pineapple, cubed
extra rum for serving

Heat the oil in a pan and gently fry the onion for 5–8 minutes until soft. Add the garlic and spices and cook for 2–3 minutes. Mix in the sweet potato, courgettes and green bananas, cover and sweat for 8–10 minutes, stirring occasionally.

Add the tomato juice, lime juice and rum, plus extra stock if necessary (though the courgettes may provide enough liquid). Cover and cook for 1–1½ hours until the banana is tender and the flavours well developed. Season to taste. Garnish with spring onions and pineapple, adding an extra dash of rum before serving.

LA KAMA

This spicy bean casserole uses a combination of spices from the Middle East, where the hotness comes from ginger and black pepper and sweetness from cinnamon and nutmeg. Prepare most spiced casseroles in advance, even by one or two days, as they improve when kept and reheated. Keep the mushrooms and courgettes very chunky. Serve with rice, wild rice or bulgar wheat. For a starter, try Aubergine Dip (page 51) or Chilled Tomato and Orange Soup (page 41). Follow with fruit such as fresh pineapple, or Stuffed Dates (page 69).

SERVES 4

6oz (175g) Dutch brown or pinto beans, soaked overnight
1 tablespoon olive oil
1 leek, trimmed and finely chopped
2 cloves garlic, crushed
1 teaspoon ground cinnamon
3 teaspoons ground ginger
pinch of grated nutmeg
1 teaspoon ground black pepper
1 teaspoon ground turmeric
1lb (450g) courgettes, trimmed and thickly sliced
8oz (225g) field mushrooms, wiped and cut into quarters
1 green pepper, deseeded and sliced in strips
¼–½ pint (150–275ml) bean stock
salt or shoyu

Drain the beans and rinse well. Place in a pan, cover with plenty of fresh water and bring to the boil. Boil fiercely for 10 minutes, then cover and simmer for 35–40 minutes or until the beans are cooked. Drain, reserv-

ing the stock. Heat the oil in a pan and gently fry the leek for 5 minutes until softened. Add the garlic and cook for 2 minutes.

Mix the spices with a little of the reserved bean stock to make a soft paste. Add the paste to the leek, then fry for 2–3 minutes or until the liquid has evaporated and the spices are well cooked. Stir in the cooked beans and vegetables, mixing well, and cook for 5 minutes.

Pour on ¼ pint (150ml) of the reserved stock, bring to the boil, cover and simmer for 1 hour, checking on the liquid level and adding more stock if necessary. Season to taste before serving.

POLISH VEGETABLE FRICASÉE

Caraway and thyme work very well with vegetables, particularly the root and leaf varieties, as they provide a peppery undertone. Buttermilk adds the necessary tang to balance the mealiness of the potatoes. Serve with noodles and green vegetables or a tomato pasta.

SERVES 4

2 tablespoons sunflower oil
2 onions, peeled and finely chopped
2 leeks, trimmed and chopped
8oz (225g) white cabbage, shredded
8oz (225g) turnip, peeled and diced
12oz (350g) potato, scrubbed and diced
1 tablespoon caraway seeds
½ tablespoon dried thyme
6 allspice berries, crushed
¾oz (20g) brown rice flour
½ pint (275ml) buttermilk
1 teaspoon prepared mild mustard
salt and pepper

Heat the oil in a pan and very gently fry the onion for 5 minutes. Add the leeks, cabbage, turnip and potato, mixing well, and sweat for 5 minutes. Add 3–4 tablespoons of water, cover and cook for 15 minutes. Add the caraway, thyme and allspice berries and cook for another 5 minutes. Sprinkle over the flour and cook for 2 minutes.

Stir in the buttermilk and mustard. Gradually bring to the boil and simmer for 3 minutes or until the potatoes are tender. Season well and serve hot.

ORIENTAL MUSHROOMS AND CASHEWS

Photograph on page 86

This combination of dried and fresh mushrooms provides a rich and hearty casserole in terms of texture, colour and flavour. Add a choice of oriental vegetables – mooli, crisp textured and radish-like though not as fiery; mangetout, sweet and colourful; and pak choi, a cross between spinach and cabbage – to make a more substantial dish. Cashew nuts provide the protein. Serve with rice or noodles, or use as a filling for pancakes or stuffed vegetables.

SERVES 4

1oz (25g) dried Chinese mushrooms
¾ pint (450ml) hot water
2 teaspoons sesame oil
3 spring onions or 2oz (50g) shallots, finely chopped
½ inch (1cm) fresh root ginger, grated
1 clove garlic, crushed
4oz (110g) mooli, peeled and cubed
8oz (225g) mangetout
8oz (225g) field mushrooms
4oz (110g) cashew nut pieces
4oz (110g) pak choi or Chinese leaves, shredded
2 tablespoons rice wine or dry sherry
1–2 tablespoons shoyu
1–2 teaspoons arrowroot
pepper

Soak the dried mushrooms in the hot water for 5–6 hours. Drain well, reserve the stock and thinly slice the mushrooms.

Heat the sesame oil in a pan and fry the onions or shallots for 5 minutes, then add the ginger and garlic and cook for 1 minute. Mix in the mooli, mangetout, mushrooms, nuts and sliced dried mushrooms. Cover and cook for 8–10 minutes, stirring occasionally. Add the pak choi, wine and shoyu.

Dissolve the arrowroot in ½ pint (275ml) of the reserved mushroom stock and stir into the vegetables. Bring to the boil, stirring frequently, until the sauce thickens and clears. Season to taste and serve immediately.

CURRIES

We have adopted the term 'curry' to describe all sorts of spiced dishes that come principally from India and Far Eastern countries, but in fact the combinations of spice mixtures are endless and vary from region to region, or indeed from family to family. Spices are very important as flavouring ingredients of vegetarian foods, providing different aromas as well as visual appeal with red or golden colourings. Try to buy whole spices, grinding them fresh as required. Remember that spices should be cooked to release their fragrance and to improve their digestibility, and they are more powerful if lightly crushed or ground. When using ground spices, it is easier to mix them into a paste with water before cooking. The water will be driven off and the spices will not burn and become bitter. If using whole spices in an uncooked dish, it is best to dry roast them first in a heavy pan.

I have suggested two spice mixtures in the following recipes. One is a fragrant blend – based on the classic garam masala – using spices which are aromatic rather than hot and fiery. This mixture combines particularly well with dishes using dairy products such as yoghurt or cheese, as well as mixtures of vegetables with fruit added. The lentil recipe is a hotter mixture which complements the floury taste of pulses. Both these curries can be served with rice or bread, or in smaller quantities to accompany drier dishes such as grain or vegetable bakes.

RED KIDNEY BEAN CURRY

Curries do not always have to be fiery hot or Indian in style. This bean curry comes from southern Asia and has the combination of flavourings typical of that area – garlic, ginger, lemon and creamed coconut. The richness of the sauce complements the dry floury nature of the beans, and the ground nuts add extra texture. Although very quick to cook, this curry will be better if you make it in advance, allow the flavours to develop and then reheat it. Serve with rice or millet, with chopped tomatoes or cucumbers as an accompaniment.

SERVES 4

6oz (175g) red kidney beans, soaked overnight
1 red chilli
1 slice of fresh root ginger
1 teaspoon grated lemon rind
2 tablespoons chopped coriander root or lower stems
1 clove garlic, crushed
½ teaspoon ground pepper
3 tablespoons grated creamed coconut
3oz (75g) roasted peanuts, ground
⅓ pint (200ml) coconut milk
1 red pepper, deseeded and finely diced
juice of ½ lemon
salt and pepper
Garnish
2–3 tablespoons chopped fresh coriander

Drain the beans and rinse well. Place in a pan with plenty of fresh water and bring to the boil. Boil fiercely for 10 minutes, then simmer for 30–40 minutes or until the beans are cooked. Drain.

Crush the chilli, ginger, lemon rind, coriander stem, garlic and pepper in a pestle and mortar to make a stiff paste. Dissolve the creamed coconut in 1 tablespoon boiling water to make a thick cream. Heat the cream in a small pan until it bubbles and separates slightly. Add the spice paste and cook for 3–4 minutes. Stir in the peanuts and cooked beans. Pour over the coconut milk, stir in the red pepper and cook for 10 minutes, stirring frequently. Add the lemon juice and season to taste. Serve garnished with chopped coriander.

FRAGRANT VEGETABLE CURRY

Photograph on page 87

SERVES 4

1 tablespoon sunflower oil
1 onion, peeled and finely chopped
1 clove garlic, crushed
½ teaspoon ground cardamom
¼ teaspoon ground cinnamon
½ teaspoon ground cumin
½ teaspoon ground coriander
pinch of cloves
3 tablespoons water
8oz (225g) green beans, trimmed and sliced
8oz (225g) cauliflower florets
8oz (225g) button mushrooms, wiped and halved
½ pint (300ml) natural yoghurt
1 teaspoon wholewheat flour
2fl oz (50ml) water
1 tablespoon tomato purée
1 tablespoon chopped fresh coriander
salt and pepper

Heat the oil in a pan and gently fry the onion and garlic for 4–5 minutes until soft. In a small bowl, mix the spices together with the 3 tablespoons water to make a paste. Add to the pan and fry for 30 seconds or until the mixture looks dry. Add the vegetables, stir well and cook for 5 minutes. Mix the yoghurt with the flour and water and add to the pan with the tomato purée. Bring slowly to the boil, cover and simmer for 45–50 minutes, stirring occasionally and adding more water if necessary. Just before serving, stir in the coriander and season to taste.

SPICED LENTIL AND VEGETABLE CURRY

SERVES 4
2 tablespoons sunflower oil
1 onion, peeled and finely chopped
1–2 cloves garlic, crushed
1 teaspoon cumin seeds
1 teaspoon coriander seeds
1/2 teaspoon mustard seeds
1/4 teaspoon fenugreek seeds
1/4 teaspoon ground turmeric
1/4 teaspoon chilli powder
1/2 teaspoon grated fresh root ginger
1lb (450g) courgettes, trimmed and diced
1 medium aubergine, cubed
4oz (110g) red lentils, cleaned and rinsed
1 × 14oz (400g) tin of tomatoes, puréed
1/2 pint (275ml) water
salt and pepper
lemon juice for serving (optional)

Heat the oil in a large pan and cook the onion and garlic for 4–5 minutes until just softened. Add the seeds, turmeric and chilli powder with a little water. Stir in the ginger and cook for 1–2 minutes until the seeds are lightly roasted. Add the courgettes and aubergine and cook for 5 minutes. Mix in the lentils and cook for 1 minute. Pour over the tomatoes and water.

Bring the curry to the boil, cover and simmer for 35–45 minutes or until the lentils and vegetables are well cooked. Check on the liquid content from time to time and add more water if necessary. Adjust the seasoning before serving and add lemon juice if liked.

TANDOORI TOFU AND POTATO CURRY

Strictly speaking, tandoori cooking refers to food that is baked, roasted and grilled simultaneously in a tandoor – an Indian oven. But often the ingredients are marinated in spiced yoghurt first, and this is what I have done here, substituting a frying pan for the tandoor. Any form of marinating is suitable for tofu, as it is able to soak up the flavours. Potatoes, too, have a neutral taste that absorbs flavourings, so these two ingredients form a good basis for the curry. Serve this rather dry curry with a bread or rice, and possibly with some moist and colourful vegetables and a salad with Yoghurt Dressing (page 180).

SERVES 2 AS A MAIN DISH OR 4 AS AN ACCOMPANIMENT

2 cloves garlic, crushed
1 tablespoon grated fresh ginger root
1 teaspoon cumin seeds, roasted
½ teaspoon cardamom seeds
1 teaspoon paprika
4fl oz (110ml) natural yoghurt
8oz (225g) firm tofu, cubed
8oz (225g) potatoes, boiled
1–2 tablespoons sunflower oil
Garnish
fresh coriander leaves

For the marinade paste, crush the garlic, ginger, cumin, cardamom and paprika in a pestle and mortar to a fine paste. Stir in the yoghurt.

Put the cubes of tofu in a shallow dish and coat with marinade. Leave for at least 2 hours or longer if possible.

Cut the potatoes into bite-sized cubes. Heat the oil in a large frying pan and gently fry the potatoes for 4–5 minutes until lightly browned. Drain the cubes of tofu, add to the pan and fry for 3–4 minutes, mixing well with the potatoes, and then remove the mixture from the pan. Gradually add the marinade to the pan, stirring in 1 tablespoon at a time, so that the mixture does not curdle. Return the tofu and potato cubes to the pan and heat through. Garnish with fresh coriander and serve hot.

GRATINS
& BAKES

The word 'gratin' literally means 'food burnt on top'. More appetising is the thought of creamy textures, golden tops of melted cheese, crispy breadcrumbs and white sauces. Gratins are both satisfying to eat and easy to prepare. Before I became completely vegetarian, I often used to make quick midweek suppers from mixtures of cooked vegetables either left chunky or puréed and then smothered in sauce, topped with cheese and grilled. Its simplicity was appealing and we nicknamed it 'earthfood'. But you needn't just have gratin-style dishes made from dairy products; soya milk with its nutty flavour can be used. Dilute soya milk slightly as you will find sauces made from it tend to be thicker. You can use soya milk in a plain white sauce or vary it using yeast flakes for a cheesy flavour. Split pea or lentil purées such as the one on page 128 are also good alternatives to dairy-based sauces.

Other alternatives to dairy milk are nut milks. They are easy to make using a blender or food processor. The best results are obtained from almonds or cashews. Again, watch out that they do not become too thick or the end result can be cloying.

For a final touch, add a simple crumble topping, toasted nuts and seeds, or fresh herbs. All these give the recipe a more finished appearance as well as making it more sustaining. Another way of making dishes like these more substantial is to add a croustade base. This is like an upside-down crumble, made from mixtures of flakes, breadcrumbs, nuts and, sometimes, cheese. The original term meant a fine shell of toasted bread, but I find the crumble case less fragile. The Cauliflower and Walnut Croustade uses a crunchy pizza style vegetable and tomato topping with a flavoured base. A similar idea could be used for virtually any mixture of sauce and vegetables providing it is thick enough. The firmer the texture, the easier it is to cut and serve.

Gratins needn't just be seen as homely fare. Depending on the choice of vegetables and the richness of the sauce, you can make sumptuous dinner party dishes. Try the Layered Vegetable Fondu, where the vegetables are baked in a wine sauce, or Vegetables à la Cloche with a delicious soured cream topping.

I have also included a delicious Carrot and Courgette Bake, with a light texture and most appealing combination of colours, which will be firm enough to cut in slices and can be made more substantial by encasing in pastry.

CREAMY VEGETABLE CRUMBLE

This homely recipe is an example of how to use a sauce as the basis for a more robust meal. Vegetables served this way are easy to prepare but can lack focus on the plate, giving the impression that something is missing. Adding a crumble topping is a quick way of providing a finish, extra texture and fibre and makes the meal easy to present. Choose an attractive oven-to-table dish. Serve this meal on its own, with a salad as a starter, accompanied by small bowls of toasted seeds, chopped nuts, herbs or grated cheese as a garnish. Alternatively, choose a jacket potato or cooked grain or pasta for a substantial accompaniment, or just a simple vegetable as a contrast to the rest of the meal.

SERVES 4

1¼ pints (700ml) Green Split Pea Sauce (page 128)
1½–2lb (700–900g) mixed root vegetables, eg parsnip, carrot, swede
salt and pepper
Crumble Topping
2oz (50g) wholewheat flour
1oz (25g) wheatgerm
2oz (50g) porridge oats
2oz (50g) sunflower seeds
1oz (25g) yeast flakes
1oz (25g) sunflower margarine

Preheat the oven to Gas Mark 4, 350°F (180°C). Prepare the sauce (see page 128) and set aside. Scrub or peel the vegetables and cut into bite-sized pieces. Steam for 8–10 minutes or until tender. Season well. Mix the vegetables and sauce together and transfer to a large ovenproof dish.

For the topping, mix all the dry ingredients together thoroughly, then rub in the margarine until fairly well distributed. Sprinkle the crumble over the top of the vegetables and press down lightly. Bake for 20–25 minutes or until golden brown. Serve hot.

GREEN SPLIT PEA SAUCE

This is a rich creamy sauce, useful for a whole variety of occasions, but especially when you want to avoid dairy products. White sauces made from soya milk are fairly rich as the soya bean does contain some fat. You can buy several types of soya milk. Some are plain, others have sugar added and are best for sweet sauces. Concentrated soya milk is also available and can be used neat as a topping in place of cream or yoghurt, or diluted for a sauce. In this recipe, cooked and puréed green split peas provide the colour and flavour as well as extra protein.

MAKES 1¼ PINTS (700ML)
4oz (110g) green split peas, rinsed
¾oz (20g) sunflower margarine
¾oz (20g) wholewheat flour
1 pint (570ml) soya milk
1 tablespoon yeast flakes
1 teaspoon dried sage
1 teaspoon dried rosemary
salt and pepper

Put the green split peas in a pan with plenty of fresh water. Bring to the boil, cover and simmer for 40 minutes. If you are using a pressure cooker, cook for 15 minutes. Drain the peas and mash well.

For the sauce, gently melt the margarine in a medium pan. Sprinkle over the flour, stir in to make a roux and cook for 1–2 minutes. Gradually add the soya milk, stirring continuously until smooth. Bring to the boil and simmer for 2–3 minutes, stirring frequently. Add the mashed peas, yeast flakes and herbs. Cook for 2–3 minutes, then season to taste.

ALMOND AND BROCCOLI GRATIN

Sauces made with ground nuts make a good creamy base for a vegetable dish when you want to serve a rich dish but prefer not to use dairy products. Almonds, cashews and peanuts are the best nuts to use. Walnuts and hazelnuts tend to be a little overpowering and Brazil nuts are too fatty. When making nut sauces, remember they will thicken on standing, so have some extra stock available to dilute the mixture if necessary. I prefer to add vegetables to the sauce as I find the flavour more rounded.

The vegetables included in the gratin itself can be varied according to the season. Always try to have a mixture of colours and textures. This recipe is a good combination for the winter; in summer, French beans, runner or broad beans would work well, as would baby white turnips or artichoke hearts. You could also use carrots, fennel or celeriac.

SERVES 4
2 tablespoons sunflower oil
1 medium onion, peeled and finely chopped
2 sticks of celery, trimmed
4oz (110g) ground almonds
1 pint (570ml) vegetable stock
2–3 tablespoons finely chopped fresh parsley
2oz (50g) bulgar wheat
1lb (450g) broccoli florets
8oz (225g) Jerusalem artichokes, peeled and diced
4oz (110g) carrots, peeled and grated
juice of ½ lemon
2 tablespoons water
salt and pepper
Garnish
2oz (50g) flaked almonds, toasted
parsley sprigs

For the sauce, heat 1 tablespoon of the oil in a pan and gently fry the onion for 4–5 minutes. Stir in the celery and cook for 3 minutes. Add the ground almonds, stirring in well as they will absorb the oil and may stick to the bottom of the pan. Cook for 2–3 minutes, then pour over the vegetable stock and add the parsley. Bring to the boil, stirring occasionally, cover and simmer for 10 minutes.

Remove the pan from the heat, allow to cool slightly, then purée in a blender or food processor until smooth and creamy. Add the bulgar and cook for 8–10 minutes until the bulgar has swelled and softened.

Meanwhile, heat the remaining oil in a pan and quickly stir fry the broccoli and artichokes for 2–3 minutes. Stir in the carrots and cook for 1 minute, then add the lemon juice and water. Season to taste. Cover and braise the vegetables for 3–4 minutes, shaking the pan if necessary, until just tender. Cook the mixture longer if you prefer a softer texture.

Drain the vegetables if necessary, then mix into the almond sauce. Pour the mixture into a serving dish, cover thickly with toasted almonds and garnish with parsley. Serve hot.

CARROT AND COURGETTE BAKE

Photograph on page 153

This colourful vegetable bake makes a very good hot supper dish, or serve it in small squares as a lunchtime savoury or starter. The mixture of eggs and cheese gives the dish a rich taste, while the vegetables add colour. Carrots are always useful for this and they are complemented by the flecks of green courgette. You could use finely shredded cabbage or very tiny florets of broccoli or cauliflower. Add a mixture of seeds for an interesting crunchy quality without losing the essential lightness. A little shoyu with the seeds peps up the flavour. Serve with pasta or baked potatoes. This bake could also act as a foil to highly spiced dishes such as vegetable curries.

SERVES 4

1oz (25g) sunflower seeds
1oz (25g) sesame seeds
2 teaspoons shoyu
1 tablespoon sunflower oil
1 onion, peeled and finely chopped
1 clove garlic, crushed
8oz (225g) carrots, peeled and grated
8oz (225g) courgettes, trimmed and grated
4 eggs, beaten
2oz (50g) fresh wholewheat breadcrumbs
4oz (110g) Cheddar cheese, grated
1 teaspoon chopped fresh sage
salt and pepper

Preheat the oven to Gas Mark 4, 350°F (180°C). Roast the seeds in a heavy based dry frying pan for 2–3 minutes or in the oven for 10–15 minutes. Add the shoyu and mix well, then continue frying for 1 minute or roasting for 3 minutes. Leave to cool.

Heat the oil in a pan and gently fry the onion and garlic for 5 minutes until softened but not coloured. Stir in the carrots and courgettes and cook for 2 minutes. Remove the pan from the heat and mix in the roasted seeds. Stir the eggs into the vegetables with the breadcrumbs, cheese and sage. Season well.

Spoon the mixture into a lightly greased ovenproof dish. Bake for 20–30 minutes or until set. Serve hot straight from the dish, or leave until cold and cut into squares.

LAYERED VEGETABLE FONDU

This delicious and simple recipe is a far cry from an ordinary cheese and vegetable bake. Use a dry white wine and a well flavoured cheese. A little wholewheat flour makes the sauce thick and creamy, and caraway counteracts the richness. I have used leeks, parsnips and sweetcorn, but there are plenty of other vegetables that work well – potato, cauliflower, swede, kohlrabi or Jerusalem artichoke. Do not use a vegetable that gives off too much liquid as it will dilute the flavour. Another way of serving this dish as a main course would be to add a crumble or pastry topping. Alternatively, serve as a side dish with a roast or bake, or serve tiny individual portions as a starter.

SERVES 4

8oz (225g) onion, peeled and sliced in rings
8oz (225g) leeks, trimmed and roughly chopped
12oz (350g) parsnips, peeled and thickly sliced
6oz (175g) baby sweetcorn
½ teaspoon caraway seeds
generous pinch of mace
¼ pint (150ml) white wine
1½ tablespoons wholewheat flour
6oz (175g) Edam cheese, grated
salt and pepper
1oz (25g) sunflower margarine

Preheat the oven to Gas Mark 4, 350°F (180°C). Layer the vegetables in a well greased casserole, sprinkling caraway seeds and mace between some of the layers.

In a small pan, bring the wine to the boil. Quickly stir in the flour and cheese and beat well until the sauce is smooth. Season to taste. Pour this fondu sauce over the vegetables. Dot a little margarine over the top. Bake for 1 hour or until the vegetables are tender. Serve hot.

GOLDEN PIE

Golden cornmeal is used in the topping for this satisfying red kidney bean and vegetable pie. You could serve it with a tomato or cheese sauce.

SERVES 4

6oz (175g) red kidney beans, soaked overnight
1 tablespoon olive oil
1 large onion, peeled and finely chopped
2 cloves garlic, crushed
1 fresh green chilli, deseeded and chopped
1 teaspoon cumin seeds
2 green peppers, deseeded and diced
8oz (225g) celeriac, peeled and diced
1 tablespoon red wine vinegar
¼ pint (150ml) bean stock
1–2 tablespoons tomato purée
3 tablespoons finely chopped fresh parsley
salt and pepper
Topping
5oz (150g) cornmeal
1 teaspoon baking powder
½ teaspoon salt
2oz (50g) sunflower margarine
7fl oz (200ml) buttermilk

Drain the beans and rinse well. Put in a pan with plenty of fresh water. Bring to the boil and boil fiercely for 10 minutes, then cover and simmer for 25–30 minutes or until the beans are cooked. Drain, reserving the stock.

Heat the oil in a separate pan and gently fry the onion for 2–3 minutes. Add the garlic and cook for 2 minutes, taking care not to brown the onions. Add the chilli, cumin, peppers, celeriac and cooked beans and cook for 5 minutes, stirring well. Add the vinegar, reserved bean stock and tomato purée. Bring to the boil and simmer for 10 minutes until thickened. Add the parsley and season to taste. Spoon the mixture into a lightly greased ovenproof dish.

Preheat the oven to Gas Mark 6, 400°F (200°C). For the topping, mix the cornmeal with the baking powder and salt in a bowl. Melt the margarine in a small pan, then mix the margarine and buttermilk with the cornmeal, stirring well until the consistency of a thick batter. Pour the topping over the cooked beans. Bake for 20–25 minutes or until the topping is set and lightly browned.

CAULIFLOWER AND WALNUT CROUSTADE

The original idea of a croustade was a crust made of thin slices of stale bread, brushed with melted butter and baked until crisp. My less fragile version is more of a crumble topping mixture that forms a case. Once baked, the case can be used like a flan base and filled with a wide variety of savoury or indeed sweet fillings.

SERVES 4
Base
2oz (50g) cheese
2oz (50g) walnuts
4oz (110g) rye bread
2oz (50g) coarse barley or rye flakes
2 teaspoons dill weed
2 teaspoons paprika
4 tablespoons sunflower oil
Topping
1 tablespoon sunflower oil
1 onion, peeled and finely chopped
1 clove garlic, crushed
1 × 14oz (400g) tin of tomatoes
2 tablespoons tomato purée
1 teaspoon paprika
1 medium cauliflower
4–6oz (110–175g) Cheddar cheese, grated, or 2oz (50g) mixed seeds

Preheat the oven to Gas Mark 6, 400°F (200°C). For the base, grind the cheese, walnuts and rye bread together in a blender or food processor. Mix in the remaining base ingredients. Press this mixture into a deep-sided baking dish or flan dish. Bake for 15 minutes.

Meanwhile for the topping, heat the oil in a pan and gently fry the onion and garlic for 5–6 minutes until soft. Add the tomatoes, tomato purée and paprika. Leave to cook, uncovered, for 20 minutes or until fairly thick.

Divide the cauliflower into florets and steam for 6 minutes or until just tender. Mix the cauliflower into the tomato sauce. Spread the topping over the base and cover with cheese or seeds. Return to the oven and bake for about 10 minutes until the cheese has melted or the seeds are well toasted. Serve hot.

VEGETABLES À LA CLOCHE

Photograph on page 155

This sumptuous vegetable mixture is baked in a cream, egg and cheese custard. Grains such as rice, wild rice or buckwheat are ideal accompaniments. You could also serve jacket potatoes or a hot bean dish to make the meal more substantial.

SERVES 4

2 tablespoons olive oil
1 onion, peeled and finely chopped
1 clove garlic, crushed
4oz (110g) aubergine, diced
8oz (225g) courgettes, trimmed and diced
1 red pepper
1 green pepper
8oz (225g) button mushrooms, wiped and sliced
1 teaspoon paprika
1 teaspoon chopped fresh tarragon
6oz (175g) mixed cottage cheese and cream cheese
3 eggs
salt and pepper
Topping
½ pint (275ml) mixed natural yoghurt and soured cream
1 egg
juice of ½ lemon

Heat the oil in a pan and gently fry the onion and garlic for 5–7 minutes. Add the aubergine, mix in well and cook for 4–5 minutes or until the flesh just begins to soften. Stir in the courgettes and continue slowly cooking the vegetable mixture.

Preheat the oven to Gas Mark 4, 350°F (180°C). Slice 3 or 4 rings from each pepper, then dice the remaining flesh. Add the diced pepper to the vegetable mixture with the mushrooms, paprika and tarragon. Cook for 10 minutes, stirring well until the vegetables are soft but not mushy. Remove the pan from the heat and leave to cool.

Beat the cheese and eggs together thoroughly, pour over the vegetables and mix well. Season to taste. Spoon into a well greased ovenproof dish. Bake for 10 minutes until just set.

Meanwhile for the topping, beat all the ingredients together. Spread the pepper rings over the cooked vegetables, then pour over the topping. Bake for a further 30–35 minutes or until well set. Serve hot.

SAVOURY PASTRY

Making wholewheat pastry is not difficult, but I do advise practising some of the techniques a few times, varying the quantities to take into account the type of flour or shortening you are using. Coarsely milled wholewheat flour will invariably require a little more liquid. Soft margarines contain some water already, so less water is needed to draw the dough together. For wholewheat shortcrust or flaky pastry, there are a few golden rules.

↙ Work in a cool place. If you are planning pastry for a dinner party dish, make it before the kitchen becomes hot and steamy, then leave to chill in the refrigerator.

↙ Do not overhandle rubbed-in doughs. If you have not had much success by hand, try using a food processor where the rubbing-in is done in seconds, keeping the dough cooler.

↙ Add water cautiously. Use a little oil or lemon juice if you need extra liquid as these prevent the pastry from becoming brittle. Make the initial dough on the moist side, as it will dry out as it rests.

Several ingredients can be used to enrich or change the texture of pastry, such as wheatgerm, soya flour or ground nuts and seeds. It is certainly worth trying these as they improve the nutrient value of the dough and can complement your choice of filling.

There are two basic fillings for shortcrust cases in this chapter– Tarte Maison using dairy products and Creamed Tofu and Vegetable Flan omitting them – as well as a Middle Eastern filling for a sesame pastry. Flaky pastry is used for a delicious layered pie and a rich Aduki Bean and Chestnut Loaf.

I have also included a yeasted dough as it is straightforward to make and extremely easy to roll out. This particular version is flavoured with cheese and herbs, but you could make a plainer recipe. As yeasted pastry has a slightly drier texture, use it underneath pizza-style sauces or for encasing succulent fillings.

Pasties can be made from a variety of types of pastry. They are useful for packed lunches, snacks and suppers. The two pasty fillings given could all be adapted for larger pies if you wish.

Hot water crust dough is based on an entirely different technique – boiling the fat and water together before mixing in with the flour. When cooked it makes a rigid shell that will stand up. It is naturally a harder type of pastry and best eaten straight away.

Choux pastry is not difficult but needs to be made with care. It is such an attractive pastry – delicious hot or cold. The rich party eclairs recipe has a blue cheese and nut filling but you could use other soft fillings; select any of those in the pâté chapter (page 43).

As filo pastry is becoming increasingly popular, I have included a spiced nut filling to make tyropitas – the classic filled puffed triangles. I must confess that I find these mouthwatering, but speaking with my healthy hat on, they are not the sort of food to be eaten every day due to the amount of butter and oil used. Unfortunately filo pastry can only be bought made from refined flour. I have tried making wholewheat filo but found it virtually impossible to get the necessary thinness, and the end result was disappointingly tough.

SHORTCRUST PASTRY

I like wholewheat shortcrust pastry, especially if it is rolled thinly so that it bakes crisply. Now there are plenty of finely milled wholewheat flours on the market that make a good light dough. These usually need slightly less water than the coarser varieties, though more than white flour.

WHOLEWHEAT SHORTCRUST PASTRY

There are both self-raising and plain wholewheat flours on the market and I find that self-raising flour, or plain flour with baking powder, gives the pastry a lighter texture and prevents the base of a quiche or flan from becoming soggy.

MAKES 8OZ (225G) PASTRY DOUGH
4oz (110g) wholewheat flour and 1 teaspoon baking powder or 4oz (110g) wholewheat self-raising flour
pinch of salt
2oz (50g) mixed fats (half butter and half solid vegetable fat)
1 teaspoon brown sugar
3–4 tablespoons cold water
1 tablespoon oil

Preheat the oven to Gas Mark 6, 400°F (200°C). Mix the flour and baking powder with the salt in a large bowl. Then mix together the two fats on a plate and chop into pea-size pieces. Add to the flour, mixing in with a knife so that all the pieces are lightly coated before you begin rubbing in. (The coating of flour protects the pieces of fat from the warmth of your hands and keeps the whole dough cooler.) Rub the fat into the flour until the mixture resembles fine breadcrumbs.

Dissolve the sugar in 3 tablespoons of cold water and stir in the oil. Use as much of this liquid as necessary. Sprinkle evenly over the dough and stir in with a knife. The dough should come cleanly away from the bowl and form a ball. Turn out on to a lightly floured board and knead gently until the surface of the dough is smooth. Let the pastry rest for 15–20 minutes in a cool place.

ENRICHED WHOLEWHEAT SHORTCRUST PASTRY

Richer doughs are easy to make. Soya flour boosts the protein content and adds extra fat. Sunflower seeds give the dough a nutty flavour; ground almonds could be used instead, especially for sweet pastries. Other enriching ingredients are wheatgerm or dried milk powder; again, these increase the fat content of the pastry but give the dough a crumbly texture.

MAKES 8OZ (225G) PASTRY DOUGH

4oz (110g) wholewheat flour
1 tablespoon soya flour
pinch of salt
2oz (50g) vegetable fat
1oz (25g) sunflower seeds, ground
2–3 tablespoons cold water

Mix the flour, soya flour and salt together in a large bowl. Rub in the fat until the mixture resembles fine breadcrumbs. Stir in the ground sunflower seeds. Add enough water to make a fairly soft dough, mixing in with a knife. Draw the dough together with your fingers and knead gently. Wrap the dough in polythene and leave to rest in a cool place for 30 minutes.

TARTE MAISON

A good home-made flan or quiche can make a satisfying supper dish or an excellent centrepiece at a picnic or buffet. Serve with a variety of salads, rice or potatoes. I prefer to use a thickened white sauce to bind the ingredients base because it gives the filling more substance. If there is time, infuse the milk initially with onion, peppercorns, mace and a bay leaf to give a better taste. Thicken the sauce with brown rice flour because it is creamier and lighter than wholewheat. Flavour with mustard, horseradish or garlic.

Flan fillings such as this can be cooked and served without the pastry for a quick light meal.

SERVES 4
8oz (225g) wholewheat shortcrust dough (page 137)
Filling
1oz (25g) sunflower margarine
½oz (15g) brown rice flour
¼ pint (150ml) skimmed milk
pinch of mustard powder
3 eggs, beaten
2 tablespoons single or whipping cream
4oz (110g) well flavoured cheese, eg vegetarian Edam
1 large onion, peeled and finely chopped
1 green pepper, deseeded and diced
1 teaspoon dried marjoram
salt and pepper

Preheat the oven to Gas Mark 6, 400°F (200°C). Roll out the dough and use to line an 8 inch (20cm) flan tin, pressing well into the base and sides. Prick all over with a fork. Bake blind for 4 minutes. Leave to cool.

For the filling, melt ½oz (15g) of the margarine in a small pan, sprinkle over the flour and stir in. Gradually add the milk, stirring constantly. Bring to the boil and simmer for 2–3 minutes, stirring well until smooth and thick. Add the mustard powder. Leave to cool slightly, then beat in the eggs, cream and cheese.

Melt the remaining margarine in a separate pan and gently fry the onion for 4–5 minutes until soft. Add the green pepper (or vegetables of your choice) and cook for 3–4 minutes. Add the vegetable mixture to the cheese sauce. Season well with marjoram, salt and pepper.

Spoon the filling into the pastry case and bake for 25–30 minutes or until set and well browned. Serve hot or at room temperature.

CREAMED TOFU AND VEGETABLE FLAN

Tofu makes a very good filling for flans as it has a creamy consistency and will bake until firm. There is no need to bind the mixture with an egg. If you find the final texture rather soft, cook the vegetables until only just tender. Alternatively, add 1–2oz (25–50g) chopped nuts. Use firm or silken tofu for this recipe; the firmer variety will need soya milk to dilute it. One disadvantage of cooked tofu is its beige colour which does look a little unappetising. This is easily disguised by using lots of colourful vegetables in the filling or by adding a topping of seeds, chopped nuts or fresh herbs once the flan is cooked.

SERVES 4

8oz (225g) enriched wholewheat shortcrust dough (page 138)
Filling
1 tablespoon sunflower oil
1 small onion, peeled and finely chopped
2 sticks of celery, trimmed and diced
1 small green pepper, deseeded and diced
8oz (225g) small button mushrooms, wiped
8oz (225g) firm or silken tofu
3fl oz (75ml) soya milk
1 tablespoon sunflower oil
1 clove garlic, crushed
1 teaspoon shoyu
salt and pepper

Preheat the oven to Gas Mark 6, 400°F (200°C). Roll out the dough and use to line an 8 inch (20cm) flan tin, pressing well into the base and sides. Prick all over with a fork. Bake blind for 4 minutes.

For the filling, heat the oil in a pan and gently fry the onion for 4–5 minutes. Add the celery, pepper and mushrooms and cook for 7–10 minutes, stirring occasionally.

Liquidise the tofu with the soya milk, sunflower oil, garlic and shoyu using a blender or food processor until fairly smooth. Season well. Pour this mixture over the vegetables, then transfer to the pastry case. Bake for 25–30 minutes. Serve warm.

SESAME AND AUBERGINE FLAN

A crunchy sesame pastry complements a smooth lentil filling enriched with aubergine purée. Tahini (sesame seed butter) thickens the filling as well as adding an extra nutty flavour. Don't overcook a flan filled with a lentil or other pulse purée as it will become dry and crusty and may well split open. It is best to undercook slightly so the filling remains soft. Accompany with a chunky salad, particularly Artichoke and Asparagus Salad (page 178). If you wish, use this filling with little tartlets for cocktail savouries or appetisers.

SERVES 4
Pastry
4oz (110g) wholewheat flour
pinch of salt
2 tablespoons sesame seeds
2oz (50g) vegetable fat
1 tablespoon sunflower oil
2–3 tablespoons cold water
Filling
2 large aubergines
4oz (110g) red lentils, picked over and rinsed
½ pint (275ml) water
3–4 tablespoons tahini
juice of ½ lemon
1 clove garlic, crushed
4 tablespoons chopped fresh parsley
2 tablespoons chopped fresh mint
shoyu to taste
Garnish
3–4 tablespoons mixed sesame seeds and chopped fresh parsley

For the pastry, mix the flour, salt and sesame seeds together. Rub in the fat until the mixture resembles fine breadcrumbs. Add the oil and enough cold water to make a soft dough. Knead lightly until smooth, then wrap the dough in polythene and leave to rest in the refrigerator for 30 minutes.

Meanwhile for the filling, preheat the oven to Gas Mark 4, 350°F (180°C). Bake the aubergines for 30 minutes or until soft. Slice in half, scoop out the flesh and purée in a blender or food processor.

Place the lentils in a pan with the water. Bring to the boil, cover and

simmer for 20 minutes, stirring frequently, until the water has been absorbed and the lentils are soft. Check the water level and add more if necessary but do not let the mixture become sloppy.

Add the cooked lentils to the aubergine purée with all the remaining ingredients and purée again until smooth and thick. Season to taste.

Increase the oven temperature to Gas Mark 6, 400°F (200°C). Roll out the pastry and use to line an 8 inch (20cm) flan tin, pressing well into the base and sides. Prick all over with a fork. Bake blind for 4 minutes.

Place the purée into the pastry case. Bake for 35–40 minutes. Do not overcook as the mixture will become crusty, remember that it will firm up as it cools. Sprinkle the top with sesame and parsley.

FLAKY PASTRY

This is a particularly useful pastry for special fillings because of its richness, but it is also good for pasties as it is delicious both hot and cold. I prefer to add a little rye flour to the mixture as its dry quality counteracts the high proportion of fat used. The method I use of grating in the fat certainly speeds up the process. Once this is done, you can freeze the dough until ready to use, or freeze when rolled and folded. These advance preparations make the recipe quicker to assemble.

POTATO AND SPINACH PIE
WITH GOAT'S CHEESE

A filling containing potato certainly needn't be homely, as shown by this recipe. Indeed it is a good vegetable to use as it will absorb some of the liquid created by the other ingredients and so prevent the pie from becoming soggy. A less exotic version can be made with a plain onion sauce, adding more cheese. However, whatever filling you choose, make sure the vegetables are well flavoured with herbs or spices as these counteract the richness of the pastry.

SERVES 4

Flaky Pastry
7oz (200g) wholewheat flour
1oz (25g) rye flour
½ teaspoon salt
5oz (150g) solid vegetable fat, frozen for 30 minutes
1 tablespoon lemon juice
4–5fl oz (110–150ml) cold water
Filling
½oz (15g) sunflower margarine
6oz (175g) onion, peeled and finely chopped
8oz (225g) spinach, washed
6oz (175g) button mushrooms, wiped and sliced
1 teaspoon cumin seeds
1 teaspoon dried thyme
2 tablespoons tomato purée
salt and pepper
1lb (450g) potatoes, scrubbed
2 eggs
8oz (225g) creamy goat's cheese
1 egg, lightly beaten

For the pastry, mix the wholewheat and rye flours with the salt in a large bowl. Grate in the solid vegetable fat. Add the lemon juice and enough water to bind the mixture into a rough dough. Wrap the dough in cling film or greaseproof paper and chill while preparing the filling.

For the filling, melt the margarine in a pan and gently fry the onion for 4–5 minutes. Add the spinach and mushrooms and stir fry for 2–3 minutes over a low heat until the spinach wilts. Add the cumin and thyme, cover and cook for about 5 minutes, stirring occasionally. Remove the pan from the heat and stir in the tomato purée. Season well.

Boil the potatoes in a pan of salted water for about 20 minutes. Drain well, slice and set aside. Using a blender or whisk, beat the eggs and cheese together until smooth and creamy. Season to taste.

Preheat the oven to Gas Mark 7, 425°F (220°C). To assemble the pie, roll out the dough to a long oblong, then fold in the bottom third, then the top third. Seal the edges and make a quarter turn. Repeat this. If time permits, chill the dough for a further 30 minutes. Roll out two-thirds of the dough and use to line a 9 inch (23cm) pie dish. Put in a layer of potato, then spinach mixture and pour over the beaten eggs and cheese. Repeat these layers once or twice more.

Roll out the remaining pastry and use as a lid. Seal the edges with water, then pinch firmly together. Roll out any trimmings to make decorations. Brush with beaten egg and salt to glaze, then prick well. Bake for 20 minutes, then reduce the oven temperature to Gas Mark 5, 375°F (190°C) and bake for a further 30–40 minutes or until the pastry is golden brown and slightly shrinking from the edge of the dish. Serve hot or cold with a mushroom or tomato sauce, or with Watercress Sauce (below).

WATERCRESS SAUCE

Accompany Potato and Spinach Pie with Goat's Cheese (above) with this sauce, in which the slightly peppery taste of watercress works particularly well with the spinach and cheese filling.

SERVES 4
1oz (25g) sunflower margarine
1oz (25g) wholewheat flour
1 pint (570ml) milk, infused with ½ onion, 1 bay leaf and 6 peppercorns
1 large bunch of watercress, washed
salt and pepper

Melt the margarine in a small pan, sprinkle over the flour and cook over a gentle heat for 1–2 minutes, stirring until smooth. Add one third of the milk, stirring well, then add the remaining milk, mixing well. Gradually bring the sauce to the boil, stirring constantly, and simmer for 3–4 minutes. Cool slightly, then liquidise with the watercress in a blender or food processor. Season to taste. Reheat gently before serving.

ADUKI BEAN AND CHESTNUT LOAF

Photograph on page 154

The flaky pastry crust in this recipe surrounds a mixture full of rich flavours and colours. Although aduki beans, chestnuts and red peppers are all sweet, the Tabasco and wine vinegar add a balancing tang. Pulses are useful for roasts and bakes as they have a good floury texture and provide a substantial base. However, the earthy flavour needs to be made more interesting with vegetables either cooked well or puréed, and

herbs and spices. Use nuts for richness. I have also tried this mixture baked without the crust; it works well but can be a little fragile to cut while hot, so add an egg to the mixture for easier slicing.

SERVES 4
6oz (175g) dried aduki beans, soaked overnight
4oz (110g) dried chestnuts, soaked for 1 hour
2 large red peppers
1 tablespoon olive oil
4 cloves garlic
2 teaspoons wine vinegar
2 tablespoons tomato purée
2 teaspoons dried oregano
4oz (110g) fresh wholewheat breadcrumbs
1/2–1 teaspoon Tabasco sauce
4 tablespoons shoyu
2 tablespoons red wine vinegar
salt and pepper
flaky pastry, made with 7oz (200g) wholewheat flour (page 142)
1 egg, beaten

Drain the beans and rinse well. Put in a pan with plenty of fresh water. Bring to the boil and boil fiercely for 10 minutes, then simmer for 35–40 minutes or until tender. Drain the beans and mash.

Meanwhile, cook the chestnuts in their soaking liquid for 50–60 minutes or until tender. Drain and grind the chestnuts in a blender or food processor.

Preheat the oven to Gas Mark 5, 375°F (190°C). Bake the peppers for 20–25 minutes or until the skins are charred. Cool and skin the peppers. Finely dice the flesh. Heat the oil in a pan and cook the peppers and garlic over a very gentle heat, covered, for 15 minutes. Add the vinegar, tomato purée and oregano, then mix in the aduki beans and chestnuts. Add the breadcrumbs, Tabasco, shoyu and red wine vinegar. Stir well, then season to taste. The mixture should be moist but not sloppy.

Increase the oven temperature to Gas Mark 7, 425°F (220°C). Roll out the pastry to a large oblong and place the filling along one side. Fold the remaining pastry over the filling and seal well with a few drops of water. Trim off any extra pieces and use to decorate the loaf. Place the loaf on a baking sheet and brush with beaten egg. Bake for 20 minutes, then reduce the heat to Gas Mark 5, 375°F (190°C) and cook for a further 30–40 minutes. Serve hot with a tomato sauce.

YEASTED PASTRY

This type of dough is a cross between bread and pastry. It is simple to make with either fresh or dried yeast and is particularly easy to roll out. Anyone new to wholewheat flour may find ordinary pastry rather tricky to handle at first but a yeasted dough is generally more manageable and just as quick to make. It is not necessary to leave the dough to rise for any great length of time. Another advantage of a yeasted dough is that it is healthier as it uses fewer fats.

FOLDED PIZZAS

Transporting a pizza for a picnic or packed lunch can be disastrous as it will invariably get turned upside down. The solution is to fold the filling in a pastry case. This pastry dough includes cheese, herbs and other flavourings, but it can also be made plain.

MAKES 8 PIZZAS
Yeasted Pastry
1lb (450g) wholewheat flour
½ teaspoon salt
¾oz (20g) fresh yeast
1 tablespoon clear honey
½ pint (275ml) warm water
1 tablespoon soya flour
1 tablespoon olive oil
1 tablespoon dried oregano
1 tablespoon dried thyme
2oz (50g) Cheddar cheese, grated
Filling
1 tablespoon olive oil
1 large onion, peeled and finely chopped
1 clove garlic, crushed
8oz (225g) field mushrooms, wiped and finely sliced
2–3 tablespoons tomato sauce
1–2 tablespoons black olives, finely diced
salt and pepper
6oz (175g) Cheddar cheese, grated

For the yeasted dough, mix the flour and salt together in a large bowl. Cream the yeast and honey together in a small bowl and add ¼ pint (150ml) of the warm water. Whisk until the yeast is dissolved, then leave in a warm place for 5 minutes until the surface is frothy.

Pour the yeast mixture over the flour, add the remaining water, the soya flour, oil and herbs. Draw up the dough to a rough ball and knead thoroughly until smooth and elastic. Put the dough into a clean bowl, cover with cling film or a damp cloth and leave for 30 minutes.

Meanwhile for the filling, heat the oil in a pan and gently fry the onion and garlic for 7–10 minutes, stirring frequently, until soft but not coloured. If the mixture seems a little dry add 1–2 tablespoons water. Add the mushrooms and cook for 5 minutes until softened. Stir in the tomato sauce and olives. Cook, uncovered, for 10–15 minutes until moist and rich. Season to taste.

Knock back the dough and knead in the cheese. To assemble the pizzas, divide the dough into 8 pieces – each of these should weigh between 3–4oz (75–110g). Roll out each piece into a small round, the size of a tea plate. Divide the filling between the rounds of dough and sprinkle with cheese. Fold each round in half and seal with water. Place on a greased baking sheet, cover with a cloth and leave in a warm place for 15 minutes.

Meanwhile, preheat the oven to Gas Mark 7, 425°F (220°C). Bake the pizzas for 15–20 minutes. Eat hot or cold.

HOT WATER CRUST PASTRY

In Elizabethan times, this pastry was used as a shell for transporting ingredients, or as a throw-away plate. Hot water crusts are spectacular cases and easy to make too. My first vegetarian Christmas dinner featured this type of pie and was very successful. You can devise all sorts of fillings which work well. Do not choose anything too liquid or it will soften the pastry too much and will collapse once unmoulded. Prepare the filling in advance as you need to work with the pastry while it is hot.

When making the dough, make sure the water and fat are boiling. Use a wooden spoon to stir in the liquid initially then, as soon as you can, knead by hand, watching out for trapped pockets of hot liquid. Have ready some extra boiling liquid in case the dough is too dry.

The best type of tins to use are spring sided moulds, either plain or fluted, as these open so that you can slide the pie out easily. Cake tins, loaf tins and individual dishes such as ramekins do not have to be greased, but the pastry will not turn out unless it is thoroughly cooked.

Hot water crust pastry can be eaten hot or cold. If you use a great deal of water in the dough it may become rather tough when cool. Practice to get the right consistency. However, as with the Elizabethans, it is an excellent way to carry moist fillings for a picnic or lunch box.

LAYERED CHEESE AND VEGETABLE PIE

SERVES 4
Filling
1oz (25g) sunflower margarine
1oz (25g) wholewheat flour
½ pint (275ml) milk, infused with ½ onion, few peppercorns and 1 bouquet garni
4oz (110g) mixed chopped nuts, eg hazels and walnuts
1½ teaspoons dried sage
½ teaspoon dried marjoram
grated nutmeg
2 small leeks
4oz (110g) French beans
8oz (225g) cauliflower
4oz (110g) Cheddar cheese, grated
salt and pepper
Hot Water Crust Pastry
12oz (350g) wholewheat flour
pinch salt
4oz (110g) solid vegetable fat
4fl oz (110ml) water
1 egg, lightly beaten

For the filling, melt the margarine in a medium pan and sprinkle over the flour. Cook for 1 minute, stirring until smooth. Strain the infused milk and add to the pan, stirring constantly. Bring to the boil and simmer for 3–4 minutes, stirring well. Remove the pan from the heat and add the chopped nuts, ½ teaspoon of the sage, the marjoram and a generous grating of nutmeg.

Chop all the vegetables into small, even pieces. Steam lightly for 8–10 minutes until firm but just tender. Mix in the remaining sage and cheese. Season to taste.

Preheat the oven to Gas Mark 7, 425°F (220°C). For the pastry, mix the flour and salt together in a large bowl. Melt the vegetable fat and water together in a small pan until boiling fiercely. Pour immediately over the flour, mixing in quickly with a wooden spoon. As soon as possible, knead lightly with your hands to draw up the dough to a smooth ball. If dry, add more hot water. Use two-thirds of the dough to line a 7 inch (18cm) spring clip mould or deep cake tin. Press firmly into the base, and carefully work up the sides so that the walls of the pie are fairly thin.

Spread the nut sauce around the base and sides of the pie, reserving some for the top. Pack the cheesy vegetables into the centre and cover with the remaining nut sauce. Press or roll out the remaining pastry to make a lid. Pinch the sides and top firmly together. Brush the top with beaten egg, then prick well.

Bake for 20 minutes, then reduce the oven temperature to Gas Mark 5, 375°F (190°C) and cook for 45–50 minutes or until the pastry is well cooked and has shrunk from the sides. Leave in the tin for 10 minutes before unmoulding. Serve with a cheese or tomato sauce.

CHOUX PASTRY

Choux pastry is bedevilled with myths, rather like soufflés, but once you have tried making this pastry, it is surprisingly easy. It is simply a matter of learning a different technique. Always weigh the ingredients exactly. When making the dough, beat in as much air as possible as this will make the choux rise much better. It is also necessary to learn to judge the consistency of the finished dough: adding the final amount of egg needs care so that the mixture does not become sloppy. It should have a piping consistency. Always cook choux pastry in a hot oven and make sure the buns are baked crisply. If they are slightly undercooked, they can collapse. Once the choux are cooked, you can add a variety of fillings. Rich and creamy ones are the best and I have suggested a mixture of Roquefort and crème fraîche. Try vegetable purée fillings or thick sauces made from nuts.

ROQUEFORT ECLAIRS

For a hot main course, serve with a cheese sauce. This pastry includes grated cheese and dry mustard, but you can also bake choux pastry plain.

MAKES 12–15
Choux Pastry
¼ pint (150ml) water
2oz (50g) butter
2½oz (65g) wholewheat flour
2 small (size 6) eggs
2oz (50g) Cheddar cheese, grated
pinch of mustard powder
pepper
Filling
1oz (25g) hazelnuts
2oz (50g) Roquefort or strong-flavoured blue cheese
4–6 tablespoons crème fraîche
2 tablespoons chopped fresh parsley
Garnish
chopped hazelnuts
chopped fresh parsley

Preheat the oven to Gas Mark 7, 425°F (220°C). Place the water and butter in a small pan and bring to the boil, melting the butter.

Sift the flour on to a piece of greaseproof paper and, when the water and butter mixture is boiling, take the pan off the heat and shoot in the flour all at once. Beat immediately until the flour is incorporated and the mixture holds together and becomes glossy. Beat one of the eggs, add this to the mixture and beat thoroughly. There should be no trace of egg left. Beat the second egg and gradually add it to the mixture.

Mix in the grated cheese, mustard powder and pepper. Lightly grease an eclair tin and fill with the choux mixture. Bake for 20 minutes, then reduce the temperature to Gas Mark 5, 375°F (190°C). Bake for a further 5–10 minutes or until crisp. Make slits in the sides, then leave to cool.

For the filling, roast the hazelnuts under the grill or in a heavy frying pan for 3–4 minutes. Rub off the skins and finely chop the nuts. Cream the cheese with the crème fraîche until smooth. Add the chopped nuts to the cheese mixture, then stir in the parsley and a little pepper.

Fill the choux eclairs just before serving. Split them open, if necessary, and scrape out a little of the soft inside. Fill with 1–2 teaspoons of the cheese mixture. Press to close and garnish with nuts and parsley.

FILO PASTRY

Filo pastry, available from delicatessens and some larger supermarkets, is very useful to keep in the freezer. Home-made versions, especially with wholewheat flour, do not work well as they cannot be rolled out thinly enough. Bought filo pastry sheets are paper thin so handle them carefully. The trick is to defrost the pastry thoroughly. If they are even slightly frozen, they will break into tiny pieces. When working with filo pastry, use one sheet at a time and keep the rest under a damp cloth to prevent drying out. Use plenty of melted butter and olive oil to brush over the exposed areas. Once you have filled the individual pastries, leave them in the refrigerator until you are ready to bake them. The same applies to a whole layered pie.

ALMOND AND RICOTTA TYROPITAS

All sorts of fillings are suitable for these filo triangles as long as they are not too moist. As you can only put a little stuffing in each pastry, choose a mixture with plenty of flavour. This almond and ricotta mixture is nicely spiced. The Curried Tofu and Spinach pasty filling (page 158) also works particularly well.

MAKES 8–10 TRIANGLES

1 tablespoon olive oil
1 onion, peeled and finely chopped
½ teaspoon ground turmeric
½ teaspoon ground cinnamon
½ teaspoon ground ginger
2oz (50g) blanched almonds
4oz (110g) ricotta cheese
1 egg
2 tablespoons finely chopped fresh parsley
salt
2oz (50g) butter
2fl oz (50ml) olive oil
8–10 sheets of filo pastry, defrosted
Garnish
chopped fresh parsley
sesame seeds

151

Preheat the oven to Gas Mark 6, 400°F (200°C). Heat the oil in a pan and gently fry the onion for 4–5 minutes. Add the spices and cook for 2–3 minutes. Stir in the almonds and continue cooking over a gentle heat for 5 minutes, stirring. Beat the ricotta and egg together. Mix in the almond mixture and parsley. Season to taste.

Melt the butter and mix with olive oil. For each sheet of filo pastry brush with the oil mixture and fold in each of the long edges by 1 inch (2.5cm). Brush again with oil, then fold the sheet in half so that the two folded edges meet. Brush with oil again. Place a tablespoon of filling in one corner. Fold over a triangle of pastry to cover the filling, pressing down firmly, then continue folding the triangle over so that the pastry layers build up. Brush the top of the triangle and final fold well. Bake for 35–40 minutes. Do not overcook as the pastry will become crusty – remember that it firms up as it cools. Sprinkle the top with parsley and sesame seeds, then serve with natural yoghurt, if liked.

PASTIES

Pasties make a welcome change from sandwiches for packed lunches and picnics. Choose the most suitable pastry for your needs. Hot water crust should be made and eaten on the same day but is robust if you need to transport the pasty. Flaky pastry can be made well ahead of time, then frozen. It is rich and filling, and probably has the best flavour cold. Shortcrust is quick to make and useful for everyday use. The other choice is of course a yeasted dough or filo pastry.

Make the filling first, so that it has time to cool down while you prepare the pastry. Hot fillings put into cold dough make the pasties tricky to handle, as the fat starts melting. Do not try to overfill pasties as you will have problems with sealing them and the cases splitting during baking. Remember to prick the pasty to allow steam to escape. Use plain soya milk to glaze vegan pasties. These fillings are just as good in larger pies, either under a pastry crust or topped with mashed potato or a savoury crumble.

Serve hot pasties with a sauce such as those in the pasta chapter (page 71). If serving cold, have chutney, relish or mustard on hand.

Opposite: Carrot and Courgette Bake (page 130) and Creamed Celeriac (page 162)

CHEESE AND VEGETABLE PASTIES

This simple cheese and vegetable filling benefits from the flavour of fresh herbs. For a hotter taste, add a teaspoon or so of ready-made mustard.

MAKES 4–6
2 teaspoons sunflower oil
2 spring onions, trimmed and chopped
2 sticks of celery, diced
6oz (175g) carrots, peeled and diced
2 teaspoons chopped fresh sage
2 tablespoons chopped fresh parsley
4oz (110g) cottage cheese
2oz (50g) Cheddar cheese, grated
1 egg
salt and pepper
12oz (350g) wholewheat shortcrust dough (page 137) or 1 quantity flaky pastry (page 142)
1 egg, beaten

Preheat the oven to Gas Mark 6, 400°F (200°C). Heat the oil in a pan and lightly cook the spring onions for 2–3 minutes. Add the celery and carrots, cover and cook for 10 minutes over a gentle heat, stirring freqently, until the carrots are just softened. Add a little water if necessary. Mash slightly, then remove the pan from the heat and stir in the herbs, cheeses and egg. Season well.

Roll out the pastry and cut out 6 rounds, each the size of a small saucer. Fill each round with a little of the filling, then fold the pastry over and seal the edges. Brush with beaten egg and prick well. Bake for 20 minutes. If using flaky pastry, bake in the oven at Gas Mark 7, 425°F (220°C) for the first 15 minutes, then reduce the oven temperature to Gas Mark 5, 375°F (190°C) and continue baking for about 10 minutes until the pasties are cooked. Serve hot or cold.

Previous pages: Salad leaves with Light Avocado Dressing (page 181); Aduki Bean and Chestnut Loaf (page 144); farfalle (pasta butterflies) tossed in oil, garlic and sesame seeds; and Vegetables à la Cloche (page 134)
Opposite: Baked Pumpkin with Leeks and Cream (page 169); Steamed Courgettes Marinated with Mustard and Dill (page 164); and Wheat with Celery and Sunflower Seeds (page 90)

CURRIED TOFU AND SPINACH FILLING

This is an excellent way to try tofu for the first time. It gives a creamy base to the spiced spinach mixture.

FILLS 4–6 PASTIES
1 tablespoon sunflower oil
3–4 spring onions, trimmed and chopped
6oz (175g) firm tofu, finely diced
1 teaspoon curry powder
½ teaspoon ground ginger
1 tablespoon lemon juice
1 tablespoon shoyu
6oz (175g) spinach, washed and very finely shredded
pepper

Heat the oil in a pan and lightly cook the spring onions for 2 minutes. Add the tofu, curry powder and ginger and cook for 10 minutes, stirring frequently so that the tofu is broken up and the spices are well mixed in. Add the lemon juice and shoyu and cook for 1 minute. Stir in the spinach, cover and cook for 3–4 minutes until the leaves are just wilted. Season to taste, adding more lemon or shoyu if necessary. Leave to cool before filling the pasties (see page 157).

VEGETABLES

The basic staples of a vegetarian diet – pulses, grains and nuts – do not put much colour on the plate, but this can easily be remedied by adding vegetables either as an integral part of the dish or as an accompaniment. If, however, your main dish consists of many vegetables already, then keep the side dish simple, or use a cooked grain or pulse. This will also help cut down on the amount of preparation.

The quality of a vegetable is very important; choose bright, plump ones and avoid those that are bruised, wrinkled or limp. If you organise your vegetable shopping on a 2 or 3 day basis, or more frequently if possible, you will get fresher produce. If you do have to store vegetables, remove any polythene wrappings and keep in a cool dark place. This will keep them crisp and preserve light and heat sensitive nutrients. If you have a garden and access to a sudden abundance, freezing vegetables causes little loss of nutrients. Most should be blanched as this destroys the enzyme that causes deterioration. Unblanched vegetables should not be kept frozen for so long.

There are many different ways to cook vegetables; steaming, baking and stir frying are the most nutritious and will also keep the textures of the vegetables alive. An alternative form of cooking is the microwave oven which produces splendid fresh bright results. On no account steep vegetables in water for hours before cooking, and never use bicarbonate of soda. As for quantities, allow 4–8oz (110–225g) per person as a side vegetable portion.

I have covered techniques of stir frying, marinating, glazing and baking in this chapter. In some cases the recipes given for one vegetable can be adapted for another; for example, the radish recipe would also work well with turnips, the marinade for courgettes could be used for beans, mushrooms or baby artichokes. A recipe for tempura, a classic Japanese dish of assorted vegetables batter coated and deep fried in oil until crisp, is also included. Tempura makes a tasty and unusual snack or appetiser for a meal, as well as an accompaniment for a softly textured dish such as the Carrot and Courgette Bake on page 130.

Vegetables such as peppers, aubergines, courgettes, pumpkins and tomatoes are all ideal containers for stuffings. This is a very easy way to make the meal attractive and give focus to the plate. Leaves of cabbage, vines, spinach or softened leeks can be used rolled or wrapped round fillings to form interesting savoury parcels. As a change, try the more elaborate stuffed cabbage on page 171. An alternative main course could be made with cooked vegetable purées mixed with eggs, cheese or nuts to make croquettes or rissoles.

HOT BEETROOT WITH
SPICY APPLE SAUCE

Too often beetroot is confined to the salad table or the pickle jar. Many people find the precooked, pickled variety too sharp for their taste, so this splendid vegetable is often overlooked. I often use beetroot raw in a salad, where the slightly dry texture needs balancing with a fruit such as apple or orange. When served hot, a glazed sauce is ideal as it adds immediate appeal. Cream sauces go well with beetroot too, but they can be rather heavy and also go pink quite quickly so the look is spoiled. This recipe makes a splendid contrast to any main course where the predominant colour is green, such as pancakes or spinach croquettes (page 170). It also makes an unusual accompaniment to a nut or vegetable bake in place of a chutney or sauce. If you prefer a hotter version, add ginger or cayenne to the apple sauce.

SERVES 4
1–1½lb (450–700g) uncooked beetroot, trimmed
Sauce
¼ pint (150ml) apple juice
1 teaspoon fennel seeds, lightly crushed
juice of ½ orange
1 tablespoon cider vinegar
1 tablespoon tomato purée
1–2 teaspoons shoyu
1 teaspoon arrowroot

Scrub the beetroot well. Place in a pan of boiling water and simmer for 20–30 minutes or until tender. Drain and leave to cool slightly before removing the skins.

Meanwhile for the sauce, mix all the ingredients together and whisk well until the arrowroot is dissolved. Bring to the boil and simmer for 3–4 minutes until thickened and clear. Slice the hot beetroot thickly and coat with the sauce. Serve hot.

CREAMED CELERIAC

Photograph on page 153

This turnip rooted variety of the cultivated celery has a flavour like a celery heart. This recipe can be used to fill pancakes or choux pastry buns. You can make a slightly more creamy version and use it as a thick sauce for serving with Lentil and Walnut Burgers (page 65).

SERVES 4
½oz (15g) butter
1 tablespoon olive oil
1lb (450g) celeriac, prepared weight after peeling, coarsely chopped
1 clove garlic, crushed
2fl oz (50ml) white wine
2fl oz (50ml) boiling water
2–3 tablespoons smetana or soured cream
salt and pepper

Melt the butter and olive oil in a medium pan and cook the celeriac and garlic for 2–3 minutes, mixing well. Add the wine and boiling water and poach the celeriac for 10–15 minutes until most of the liquid is absorbed.

Mash the celeriac and mix in the smetana. Season to taste and serve hot or well chilled.

HONEYED RADISHES

This would go well with a grain dish such as Fruity Barley (page 93) or Potato and Spinach Pie (page 142).

SERVES 4
½oz (15g) butter
20 radishes, topped and tailed
1 teaspoon clear honey
1 teaspoon red wine vinegar
salt and pepper

Melt the butter in a pan and cook the radishes for 4 minutes. Stir in the honey and red wine vinegar, cover and cook for 10 minutes or until just tender. Season to taste and serve hot.

DEEP FRIED GREENS WITH SESAME SEEDS

This most impressive vegetable side dish is very easy to cook. Make sure the oil is hot enough and only fry about half quantity at a time, otherwise the temperature will drop and the greens will become soggy. Once fried and cooled, the shreds will crisp up and remain so for some time – several hours in fact – so this recipe does not have to be a last-minute operation. Only leaves that have a dry texture are suitable for deep frying. Chinese leaves or lettuce contain too much water and become soggy. This recipe also makes a good garnish for croquettes or rissoles, or can be used to surround a contrasting green salad.

SERVES 4

12oz (350g) spring greens or pak choi
groundnut oil for deep frying
2 tablespoons sesame seeds
salt and pepper
2 teaspoons shoyu
2 teaspoons dry sherry
2 teaspoons lemon juice
2 teaspoons orange juice
Garnish
4oz (110g) Chinese leaves, shredded
crisp lettuce leaves

Very finely shred the greens. Heat 2–3 inches (5–7.5cm) oil in a large pan and, when hot, add half the greens and stir well. Cook for 3 minutes or until quite well shrivelled. Remove from the pan with a slotted spoon and leave to drain on kitchen paper. They will crisp as they cool. Fry the remaining leaves in the same way.

For the dressing, lightly roast the sesame seeds in a small pan for 2 minutes. Cover the pan with a lid if the seeds start popping too vigorously. Grind the seeds coarsely in a pestle and mortar with a generous pinch of salt. Mix the shoyu, sherry and fruit juices together. Season lightly. Just before serving, toss this mixture with the sesame seeds into the greens. Serve on a bed of contrasting pale Chinese leaves and lettuce leaves.

STEAMED COURGETTES MARINATED WITH MUSTARD AND DILL

Photograph on page 156

A cooked side vegetable does not always have to be served hot and a marinated cold dish can be delicious. It also means you do not have the hectic last minute preparation. Any type of vegetable which has absorbent flesh is suitable – such as mushrooms, aubergines or leeks. Courgettes work well too. Slice thickly and steam until just softened so that the finished texture remains quite crunchy. I particularly like the flavour of dill with its sharp yet sweet flavour. It is a good buy dried so you can make this marinade throughout the year. For the summer though, combinations of fresh herbs could be used, for example mint and chives. This dish makes a good accompaniment to a pasta or grain dish, or for Tarte Maison (page 139) or other flans.

SERVES 4
1½lb (700g) courgettes, trimmed
1 teaspoon prepared mustard
1 teaspoon dill weed
2 tablespoons cider vinegar
1 teaspoon clear honey
4 tablespoons sunflower oil
salt and pepper

Cut the courgettes in half and slice each half into long thick slivers, or cut into thick diagonal chunks. Lightly steam for 4–5 minutes or until just tender.

In a screw-top jar, shake the mustard, dill and vinegar together thoroughly. Add the honey and oil and shake well. Season to taste.

Pour the vinaigrette over the courgettes and leave to cool. Turn over once or twice to make sure the dressing spreads through the courgettes. Serve chilled.

HERB ROASTED VEGETABLES

This is a delicious way to cook root vegetables. Leaving the marinade for a couple of hours gives the flavours a chance to develop. Alternatively, make the marinade the day before and leave overnight in the refrigerator. A rich vegetable accompaniment such as this works well with roasts or bakes or a pastry dish like Layered Cheese and Vegetable Pie (page 148). Just add a plain sauce.

SERVES 4

2lb (900g) mixed root vegetables, scrubbed or peeled
Marinade
¼ pint (150ml) olive oil
juice of ½ lemon
1 teaspoon grated lemon rind
2 tablespoons chopped fresh basil
1 tablespoon chopped fresh rosemary
2fl oz (50ml) white wine
4 cloves garlic, crushed
salt and pepper

Combine all the ingredients for the marinade in a bowl. Cover and leave to stand in a warm place for 1–2 hours.

Preheat the oven to Gas Mark 6, 400°F (200°C). Coarsely chop the vegetables uniformly. Place in a roasting dish and pour over the marinade. Bake for 1–1½ hours, basting frequently. Serve hot.

SEASONAL STIR-FRY

Although not strictly a stir-fry as some steaming is necessary to cook the root vegetables, this recipe shows that the stir-fry technique is not just confined to oriental ideas but that virtually any vegetable, except perhaps potato, can be used. It is especially useful to make this sort of dish when you have several small quantities of fresh vegetables that need to be used up. When put together as a stir-fry, you immediately get a contrast of colours and textures that will be appealing as a side dish. The seaweed in this dish makes an unusual garnish. It has a mild flavour and the dark strands are particularly effective with the vegetables.

SERVES 4

1 tablespoon groundnut oil
2 spring onions, trimmed and diced
8oz (225g) turnip, peeled and diced
8oz (225g) parsnip, peeled and diced
12oz (350g) Brussels sprouts, trimmed and halved
juice of ½ orange
1 teaspoon grated orange rind
2 tablespoons shoyu
2 tablespoons water
¼oz (7g) arame, soaked in hot water for 10 minutes
1oz (25g) sunflower seeds, toasted
salt and pepper

Heat the oil in a large wok or frying pan and fry the spring onions for 2 minutes. Add the turnip and parsnip and stir fry for 2 minutes. Stir in the sprouts and cook for 1 minute. Pour on the orange juice, rind, shoyu and water. Cover and cook for 5 minutes or until the vegetables are tender.

Drain the arame and toss it into the vegetables with the toasted sunflower seeds. Season to taste and serve hot.

TOFU AND VEGETABLE STIR-FRY

Once all the vegetables are prepared, a stir-fry is exceedingly quick to cook. With such speedy recipes, it is a problem to select a good source of protein that is equally quick to prepare and cook so that you can make it a complete meal. Tofu is ideal for this as it can be stir-fried first to give it a good flavour – or marinated ahead – and then added to the stir-fry once the vegetables are cooked so it heats through. To marinate tofu, simply use equal quantities of oil and shoyu and add flavourings such as garlic or ginger. Sharpen the mixture with lemon or orange juice and, for special occasions, add wine or sherry. Chinese five-spice powder or hot seasonings such as chillies will add a fiery quality, or use sweet fruit juices and some vinegar to make a sweet sour sauce. Depending on the type of marinade used you can always thicken it with arrowroot to make an accompanying sauce for the stir-fry. Chop the tofu into bite-sized cubes and marinate for at least 2 hours or longer for a more powerful flavour, then drain and fry. Some type of pasta or grain is needed to complete the meal. Noodles make a quick accompaniment taking 15–20 minutes to

cook, or try millet or buckwheat. However, you do not have to confine yourself to oriental ideas as this mixture could be used equally well as a pancake filling, omitting the grated carrot.

SERVES 4
2 tablespoons groundnut oil
2 cloves garlic, crushed
1 inch (2.5cm) fresh root ginger, grated
10–12oz (275–350g) firm tofu, diced
1 tablespoon shoyu
4 spring onions, trimmed and diced
6oz (175g) cauliflower, divided into florets
6oz (175g) mushrooms, wiped and sliced
6oz (175g) French beans, trimmed and diced
1 red pepper, deseeded and sliced
4 sticks of celery, trimmed and chopped
juice of ½ lemon
1oz (25g) cashew nuts, toasted
1 medium carrot, peeled and grated

Heat 1 tablespoon of the oil in a wok or large frying pan and fry the garlic and ginger for 30 seconds, taking care not to burn the garlic. Add the tofu and fry briefly, coating the cubes in the oil. Add the shoyu, stir in well. Transfer the tofu mixture to a bowl and set aside for at least 2 hours.

Heat the remaining oil in the pan and stir-fry the vegetables in the order given, frying each one for about 1 minute before adding the next variety. When all the vegetables are added, continue cooking for 3 minutes. Add the tofu and lemon juice and heat through for 2 minutes. Stir in the cashew nuts and carrot at the last minute and serve at once.

TEMPURA VEGETABLES

This deep fried vegetable dish is easy to make but it does take some time to prepare. Get the vegetables ready in advance, but do not prepare the batter and cook the vegetables until just before serving. Tempura does not have to be served just as a starter with a dip, but can make an interesting side dish for a nut roast or an addition to a buffet table. Many vegetables are suitable for deep frying in this way. Firmer vegetables such as carrots or cauliflower will not cook all the way through unless they are cut fairly small, so expect the texture to be quite crisp. Other vegetables to use are mushrooms, broccoli, courgettes, parsnip or celery. Try cooked pieces of aubergine or cubes of tofu for a soft filling. Add a pinch of cayenne to the batter to pep it up. You could add mustard, 1oz (25g) grated cheese or 1 tablespoon yeast flakes for extra flavour. Serve with a yoghurt dip, fresh tomato chutney or Rich Paprika Mayonnaise (page 178).

SERVES 6–8 AS A STARTER
2oz (50g) wholewheat flour
2oz (50g) maize meal
½ teaspoon baking powder
¼ teaspoon cayenne pepper
pinch of salt
¼ pint (150ml) water
1 egg white
sunflower oil for deep frying
1–1½lb (450–700g) vegetables, prepared and cut into small pieces

Sift the flour, maize meal, baking powder, cayenne and salt together in a bowl. Gradually add enough water to make a batter the consistency of double cream. Whisk the egg white and fold into the batter.

Heat a large pan of oil for deep frying. Dip 3–4 pieces of vegetable in the batter and deep fry for ½–1 minute. Drain on kitchen paper. Keep them warm while frying the remaining vegetables. Serve hot.

BAKED PUMPKIN WITH LEEKS AND CREAM

Photograph on page 156

Look out for baby pumpkins as they make marvellous individual tureens for this recipe. It is possible to use a large pumpkin but the presentation of the recipe will be slightly more difficult. Pumpkin flesh has a delicate flavour that combines well with the buttery quality of leeks. These, and the cream, add sufficient moisture. I find that pumpkin flesh softens easily without added water, which would dilute the taste. A similar recipe could be made with marrow except you lose the magnificent blazing colour of the pumpkin flesh. However, you could add some tomato pulp or red pepper, but do not be tempted to add water.

SERVES 2 AS A MAIN COURSE OR 4 AS A SIDE VEGETABLE

2 small pumpkins
2 tablespoons sunflower oil
1lb (450g) leeks, cleaned and diced
2 tablespoons wholewheat flour
2 teaspoons mustard powder
½ teaspoon ground mace
2 teaspoons fennel seeds
½ pint (275ml) single cream or cream and natural yoghurt mixed
1oz (25g) pumpkin seeds
salt and pepper

Preheat the oven to Gas Mark 4, 350°F (180°C). Slice a lid off the top of each pumpkin. Remove the seeds and cut out the flesh, leaving a shell. Reserve the pumpkin shells for serving. The flesh from each pumpkin should weigh about 8oz (225g). Dice the flesh.

Heat the oil in a pan and gently fry the leeks for 5 minutes. Add the pumpkin flesh and cook for 3 minutes. Stir in the flour and spices and cook for 2 minutes. Add the cream or yoghurt mixture and heat gently until the sauce thickens. Simmer for 2–3 minutes. Stir in the pumpkin seeds and season to taste.

Transfer the mixture to the pumpkin shells. Bake for 35–45 minutes or until the shells are quite soft. Serve hot.

SPINACH AND CHEESE CROQUETTES

Spinach on its own may not be a vegetable to everyone's taste, as it has a strong flavour. The larger leafed variety, often available in Greek or Cypriot grocers, has a milder taste and is easier to clean. It is a vegetable worth getting to like, not only for its nutrients but the brilliant colour as well. This is a particularly good introductory recipe to spinach as the other ingredients blend well and act as a foil to the spinach, and the purée gives the croquettes a much lighter texture. Try other vegetable purées with this basic idea. Carrots, parsnips and Brussels sprouts are all good examples. It makes a great difference to the croquettes using walnut oil as the taste is superb. Olive oil would be a fair substitute. These croquettes make an excellent accompaniment to a casserole or hot pot, as they act as a contrast to more finely chopped vegetables. Or serve them as a main course with a sauce.

MAKES 6–8

1lb (450g) spinach, washed
1–2 teaspoons walnut oil
1–2 cloves garlic, crushed
4oz (110g) Cheddar cheese, grated
6oz (175g) fresh wholewheat breadcrumbs
1–2 small (size 6) eggs, beaten
1 teaspoon caraway seeds
grated nutmeg
salt and pepper
sunflower oil for shallow frying

For the spinach purée, finely shred the spinach. Heat the walnut oil in a pan and stir fry a handful of spinach and the garlic for 1–2 minutes until the leaves become limp. Add another handful of spinach and stir fry again. Continue in this way until all the spinach is used up. Cover and cook for 2 minutes. Cool slightly and purée in a food processor or blender until smooth. Add the cheese and breadcrumbs and blend again.

Transfer the mixture to a large bowl. Gradually beat in the egg until the mixture holds together well and is fairly moist. Add the caraway and other seasoning to taste. Shape the mixture into 6–8 croquettes. (At this stage you could leave them in the refrigerator to cook later.)

Heat a little oil in a frying pan and fry the croquettes, 2 or 3 at a time, for 5 minutes, turning over during the cooking. Serve hot or warm.

LAYERED STUFFED CABBAGE

This dish makes a good meal on its own, served with potato or a strongly flavoured grain such as buckwheat. Alternatively, use it as an accompaniment to a simple pasta dish or with Bulgar Wheat Croquettes (page 62).

This unusual layered way to stuff cabbage is easy to turn out onto the serving plate. The juicy filling with its sweet yet acidic flavour sets off the taste of the cabbage. Season the mixture well and use more spices if liked.

SERVES 4–6
1 loose-leaved green cabbage, eg Savoy or January King
4oz (110g) continental lentils, picked over and washed
1 tablespoon sunflower oil
1lb (450g) leeks, cleaned and diced
1 teaspoon cumin seeds
½ teaspoon grated nutmeg
1 teaspoon dried thyme
1 tablespoon wholewheat flour
3 tablespoons red wine
2oz (50g) apricot pieces, diced
2oz (50g) raisins
salt and pepper

Slice the base off the cabbage and remove about 24 leaves. Bring a large pan of water to the boil, then blanch the leaves for 3–4 minutes until fairly soft. Drain well.

Place the lentils in a pan of fresh water. Bring to the boil and simmer for 35–40 minutes or until soft. Drain, reserving the stock, and set aside.

Heat the oil in a large frying pan and gently cook the leeks, spices and thyme for 7–10 minutes until the leeks are almost soft. Add the cooked lentils, stir in well and cook for 2 minutes. Sprinkle over the flour and cook for 1 minute. Pour over the red wine and cook until the liquid thickens slightly. Add the apricots and raisins. Season to taste.

Arrange a circle of leaves on a large muslin cloth and cover with some of the filling. Lay on more leaves and cover with more filling. Continue the layers until all the leaves and filling are used up, ending with filling. Pull the corners of the cloth together so the leaves form a ball, then tie the cloth securely.

Put the stuffed cabbage in a pan of boiling water and cook for 15–20 minutes. Remove the cloth and turn out the cabbage on to a flat plate. Serve hot, cutting the pieces in wedges, and accompany with a sauce or with soured cream and natural yoghurt blended together.

STUFFED AUBERGINES

Aubergines are excellent vegetables to stuff as the flesh has a good texture which absorbs strong flavours well. Here walnuts are used with firm tofu and plenty of refreshing lemon juice. Serve with a tomato sauce or the Spiced Yoghurt on page 92.

SERVES 4
2 medium aubergines
Filling
1 tablespoon olive oil
1 onion, peeled and finely chopped
1 clove garlic, crushed
4oz (110g) firm tofu, mashed
2oz (50g) walnuts, finely chopped
1oz (25g) oatflakes
1 teaspoon ground cinnamon
2 tablespoons tomato purée
2 teaspoons shoyu
grated rind of 1 lemon
juice of ½ lemon
pepper
Garnish
1–2 tablespoons finely chopped fresh parsley

Preheat the oven to Gas Mark 4, 350°F (180°C). Bake the aubergines for 20 minutes until slightly softened. Leave to cool, then slice each one in half lengthwise and scoop out the insides leaving a shell. Finely chop the flesh. Heat the oil in a pan and gently fry the onion and garlic for 5 minutes. Add the aubergine flesh and tofu, stir in well and fry for 5 minutes. Add a little more olive oil if the mixture begins to stick. Remove pan from heat, mix in remaining ingredients and season well.

Pile a quarter of the mixture into each aubergine, packing in well. Transfer the filled shells to a shallow baking tray and put 2 tablespoons of water around them. Cover the aubergines with foil smeared with a little oil. Bake for 30 minutes or until the outer shell is soft. Serve hot, garnished with parsley.

Opposite: Thai Fruit Salad and Mangetout and Sesame Salad (both page 186)
Overleaf: Seven Seed Bread (page 191) and Brioche Buns (page 194) with Roquefort filling (page 150)

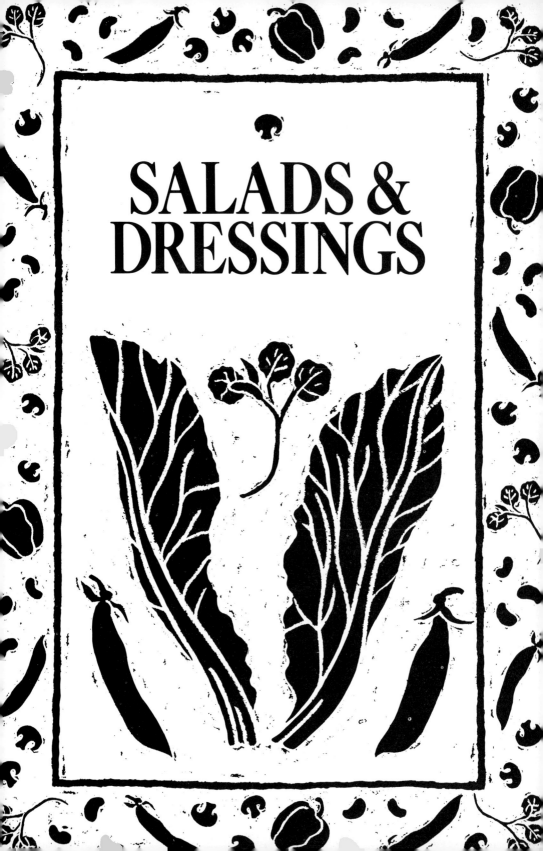

SALADS &
DRESSINGS

The salad days of limp lettuce, tasteless tomato and curling cucumber are diminishing fast, thanks to a realisation that there is a lot more to salads than the standard mixture and a great availability of ingredients, both raw and cooked, introducing a multitude of flavours and textures.

Raw food is an essential part of a healthy diet. It is high in fibre and rich in the vitamins and minerals that are so easily destroyed in the process of cooking and preserving. In fact, most vegetables can be eaten raw.

There is a wide selection of salad leaves – mild flavoured lettuce, crunchy Chinese leaves, bitter chicory, colourful radicchio and robust oak leaf, and occasionally more unusual items such as sorrel and lamb's lettuce. In addition, many root vegetables such as carrot, French turnip, celeriac and swede can be used in salads; shoots and stems like celery and fennel, as well as all the fruits and vegetable fruits such as tomatoes and avocados. You can also add nuts, seeds, dried fruits and beansprouts to salads, and all kinds of spices, seasonings and fresh herbs.

Salads are not merely side dishes. Cooked ingredients which add weight and substance, particularly grains such as rice, wheat, buckwheat and barley or pulses, make them perfect as main courses. Alternatively, add ingredients such as cubes of tofu, chunks of cheese, slices of egg to increase the protein and provide a more sustaining dish; or use hot cubes of fried bread with herb or garlic butter or cheese.

Make contrasting colourful mixtures of red kidney, green flageolet and white haricot beans, or use one particular variety.

Below are some guidelines for successful salads:

🖎 Choose a suitable dressing for the ingredients you have to hand. Fragile leafy salads will need a light dressing; finely grated ingredients should not be swamped in thick creams; chunky salads can support a heavy dressing, but very large pieces may look better with a light vinaigrette coating. Dry textured ingredients such as potatoes or pulses need a counterbalancing rich dressing using mayonnaise, cheese or nut creams.

🖎 Dress cooked salad ingredients while they are still warm, so that they will absorb the flavours while cooling.

🖎 Be selective about the salad ingredients you mix together. Think carefully about the choice of textures and colours, especially if you want to present several salads at the same meal. If they are all like rainbows, it diminishes the impact. Try choosing a theme such as the Shades of Green Salad or enliven a dull coloured ingredient with some bright fresh and dried fruit, as in the wheatgrain salad on page 183.

🖎 Don't always chop the vegetables in the same way. Root vegetables for example can be sliced into matchsticks, grated, diced or sliced; celery

can be cut on the diagonal; peppers can be sliced or cut in rings. Don't always tear leaf salads finely, as whole leaves can look very good.

✘ Always use the freshest ingredients possible. A soggy lettuce is certainly not going to crisp up in a salad bowl.

Dressings

Choose good quality oils and vinegars for dressings. These, along with herbs and seasonings, form the basis of classic vinaigrettes and oriental dressings as well as mayonnaise. Cold pressed oils have stronger flavours than the refined variety. Keep them in a cool place as they are less stable and may go rancid if exposed to constant warmth. Sunflower and safflower oils are the lightest to use. Olive oil, sold as virgin or extra virgin in its cold pressed state, has a stronger flavour; it can be used by itself or mixed with the other oils. For a change, and also a treat, try some of the more unusual oils such as hazelnut or walnut. They have most distinctive flavours and make very individual salad dressings.

I keep in stock red and white wine vinegar, cider vinegar and occasionally a flavoured vinegar such as tarragon or the delicious raspberry vinegar. They all add slightly different tastes to dressings. Start with either the cider or white wine vinegar as these are the most versatile. Other sharp ingredients which can be mixed with oils are the juices of the citrus family – lemons, limes and oranges. Use these sparingly to avoid overpowering a dressing. Mustard, tarragon and garlic can be added for a continental vinaigrette, or shoyu, sherry and ginger for an oriental touch.

There are many ways to create cream dressings using yoghurts, soft cheese, nut butters, tofu and eggs.

HERB VINAIGRETTE

SERVES 4

2 tablespoons olive oil or a mixture of olive and walnut oil
1 tablespoon lemon juice
1 teaspoon grated lemon rind
1 clove garlic, crushed
1 teaspoon French Dijon mustard
1 teaspoon chopped fresh tarragon
pinch of celery seeds
1 tablespoon finely chopped fresh parsley

Shake the ingredients together in a screw-top jar.

RICH PAPRIKA MAYONNAISE

Use paprika to add a glowing colour and mild peppery flavour to a plain mayonnaise base. It makes a good contrast to green vegetables and is a delicious savoury topping for Brioche Buns (page 194).

MAKES ½ PINT (275ML)
2 cloves garlic, crushed
1 teaspoon salt
1 teaspoon paprika
pinch of cayenne pepper
4 teaspoons lemon juice
2 egg yolks
6–8fl oz (175–225ml) mixed olive oil and sunflower oil
1 tablespoon boiling water

Mash the garlic, salt, paprika and cayenne together in a pestle and mortar. Whisk in the lemon juice and egg yolks. Add the oil drop by drop until at least 3fl oz (75ml) have been added. Whisk in the remaining oil 1 tablespoon at a time until thick. Thin down with a little more lemon juice if necessary. Lastly, add the boiling water and whisk in well.

ARTICHOKE AND ASPARAGUS SALAD

This salad goes very well with Courgette and Cheese Dip (page 49) or Rich Mushroom Rissotto (page 97).

SERVES 4
12oz (350g) baby artichokes or artichoke hearts
8oz (225g) asparagus, trimmed and coarsely chopped
8oz (225g) French beans, trimmed and halved
Herb Vinaigrette dressing (page 177)
4oz (110g) corn salad or mache
salt and pepper

If using baby artichokes, trim off the bases and any coarse outside leaves. Boil in salted water for 15 minutes or until just tender. Add the asparagus about 5 minutes before the end of the cooking time, the beans 2 minutes later, and cook until just tender. Drain well, then mix quickly into the vinaigrette. Leave to cool. When cold, toss in the corn salad. Season to taste and serve immediately.

TAHINI AND ORANGE DRESSING

Tahini is a very versatile sesame seed spread. The light version is most useful for salad dressings as it mixes easily with other ingredients. Citrus juices or apple juice both go well with the sesame flavour or use a vinaigrette dressing for a sharper taste. Once the tahini is diluted, you can add a variety of herbs and spices. Garlic always tastes good, whole aromatic seeds such as cumin or caraway and grated fresh root ginger are also fine, as well as the stronger flavoured fresh herbs such as parsley or coriander. Use this type of creamy dressing for recipes where you would normally use a thick coating mayonnaise such as a bean salad or one containing chunky vegetables.

SERVES 4
2 tablespoons tahini
4 tablespoons orange juice
1 teaspoon grated orange rind
1 teaspoon grated fresh root ginger

Mix the tahini and orange juice together to make a thick dressing the consistency of double cream. Add a little water if too thick. Stir in the orange rind and ginger. Leave to stand for 30 minutes before using.

COTTAGE CHEESE DRESSING

This is an ideal dressing for rice salads, or you could use it with coleslaw.

SERVES 4
4oz (110g) cottage cheese
2oz (50g) Cheddar cheese, grated
1 tablespoon mayonnaise
1 tablespoon cider vinegar
1 tablespoon concentrated apple juice
salt and pepper
1–2 tablespoons chopped fresh herbs, eg chives or parsley

Blend the cottage cheese thoroughly with the cheese, mayonnaise, vinegar and apple juice in a blender or food processor until fairly smooth. Add seasoning and fresh herbs to taste.

CRUNCHY ORIENTAL DRESSING

SERVES 4
3 tablespoons sesame seeds
½ teaspoon Chinese five-spice powder
2 teaspoons sesame oil
1 tablespoon sunflower oil
1 tablespoon cider vinegar
1 clove garlic, crushed
1 teaspoon clear honey

Lightly roast the sesame seeds in the oven at Gas Mark 5, 375°F (190°C) for 10–15 minutes, or under the grill or in a dry frying pan for 3–4 minutes, shaking the pan continuously. Crush the seeds with the Chinese five-spice powder in a pestle and mortar. Put the remaining ingredients into a screw-top jar, add the crushed seeds and shake well.

YOGHURT DRESSING

Yoghurt can play a very important part in creative salad dressings. It lightens rich mixtures such as mayonnaise. About 1–2 tablespoons mayonnaise to ¼ pint (150ml) natural yoghurt makes a deceptively creamy dressing. You can also combine yoghurt with blended mixtures of cottage or curd cheese, ricotta or grated hard cheese. This idea is especially useful if you are counting calories, or when you need a mild tang to complement other flavours. This yoghurt recipe also makes the basis of a pep-you-up savoury drink!

SERVES 4
½ pint (275ml) natural yoghurt
2 tablespoons tomato purée
1 teaspoon brewer's yeast
1–2 teaspoons shoyu
1–2 tablespoons chopped fresh herbs, eg basil or marjoram
salt and pepper

Blend the yoghurt with the remaining ingredients in a blender or food processor until completely smooth. Season, and use within 24 hours.

LIGHT AVOCADO DRESSING

Photograph on page 154

Avocados make an excellent base for a salad dressing as, once puréed, they act as a rich mayonnaise. You can mix avocados with soured or single cream, or a cottage or curd cheese for a lower fat version. Add lemon juice to counteract the richness and brighten the colour.

SERVES 4
1 avocado, peeled and stoned
¼ pint (150ml) soured cream or smetana
3–4 tablespoons finely chopped fresh mint
2 teaspoons lemon juice
salt and pepper

Mash the avocado flesh with the remaining ingredients and season well.

TOFU AND PEANUT DRESSING

Tofu is ideal as a creamy salad dressing. It is not just a substitute for mayonnaise but excellent in its own right. You can use either the silken or firm variety, but when blending firm tofu you will have to add extra liquid – water is fine – to dilute it to a smooth cream. Once blended, tofu can be mixed with an incredible amount of ingredients as it will absorb and complement a whole variety of flavours. Tofu is low in fat and, therefore, has a dry aftertaste. To counteract this, add an ingredient such as oil or, as in this recipe, a nut butter, so that the dressing becomes richer and works better as a salad dressing. This makes an ideal dressing for a grain salad, or for a salad made up of chunky vegetables.

SERVES 4
4oz (110g) silken tofu
2 tablespoons peanut butter
juice of ½ lemon
2 teaspoons cider vinegar
1 tablespoon concentrated apple juice
1 tablespoon sunflower oil
salt and pepper

Blend the silken tofu thoroughly in a blender or food processor until quite smooth. Blend in the remaining ingredients and season to taste.

SHADES OF GREEN SALAD

Anyone not used to eating raw vegetables may find these daunting if the pieces are too large, so cut them finely. Their strong flavour and dry aftertaste are well balanced by a rich dressing. Try other green ingredients for this salad, such as lightly steamed courgettes, French beans, fresh broad beans or peas, pak choi or Chinese leaves. This salad works well as an accompaniment for substantial main courses based on pasta or grains.

SERVES 4

1 crisp lettuce, wiped
6oz (175g) spinach, washed and finely shredded
8oz (225g) broccoli, divided into florets and chopped
Light Avocado Dressing (page 181)
Garnish
1 punnet salad cress or 2oz (50g) alfalfa sprouts

Assemble the salad ingredients. Leave small lettuce leaves whole and tear the remaining ones into large pieces. Toss the salad ingredients into the avocado dressing and transfer to a salad bowl. Garnish with salad cress or alfalfa sprouts.

POTATO SALAD

Potato salads need to be rich and creamy otherwise they can seem starchy, dry and rather hard to digest. Choose a potato that is not too floury, such as Desirée or Maris Piper.

SERVES 4

Tahini and Orange Dressing (page 179)
1lb (450g) potatoes, scrubbed or peeled
1 red pepper, deseeded and diced
1 small green chilli, deseeded and very finely chopped
3 spring onions, trimmed and diced
1oz (25g) pumpkin seeds

Make up the dressing. Place the potatoes in a pan of water and simmer for 15–20 minutes until tender. Drain well and dice the potatoes.

Mix the pepper, chilli and spring onions with the potatoes and pumpkin seeds. Stir in the tahini dressing. Serve at room temperature.

WHEATGRAIN SALAD WITH COCONUT

Cooked grains, rather like pulses, are excellent served cold in salads. They can make a complete meal, or be served with a light main course to make it more substantial. This type of salad is easy to prepare in advance, even the night before, adding any vegetables that need to be very crisp at the last minute. Rice and bulgar wheat are more frequently used in salads, but it is worth bearing in mind wheatberries or wholewheat grain work just as well. These wonderfully moist, juicy and chewy grains combine with either strong or sweet flavours. Cook enough for a hot main course so that you have left overs. Then toss a handful into a green salad or coleslaw to create an interesting texture. For an alternative dressing, try Tofu and Peanut (page 181).

SERVES 4–6

6oz (175g) wheatgrain
4oz (110g) raisins
4 sticks of celery, trimmed and diced
2 oranges, peeled and segmented
2oz (50g) creamed coconut
2fl oz (50ml) boiling water
juice of ½ lime
1 teaspoon grated lime rind
1 teaspoon grated orange rind
2 teaspoons grated fresh root ginger
1 bunch of watercress
salt and pepper

Rinse the wheatgrain if dusty. Place in a pan with plenty of cold water and simmer for 50–60 minutes or until the grains have swollen up well; a few will burst open. Drain and cool.

Assemble the raisins, celery and orange segments in a bowl and mix with the wheatgrain.

Dissolve the creamed coconut in the boiling water to make a thick cream. Add the fruit juice, rinds and ginger. Toss this dressing into the salad and leave for 1–2 hours. Just before serving, add the sprigs of watercress and adjust the seasoning.

PASTA AND CHICK PEA SALAD

Pasta makes a very useful basis for a substantial salad. It is easy to vary the appearance by using different shapes – shells, spirals or macaroni or wheat ears – and spinach pasta makes a change from wholewheat. The combination of pulses and pasta works very well, providing good protein and contrasting textures. I have suggested celery, spring onions and radicchio, but depending on what else you are going to serve with this salad, plenty of other vegetables could be added; particular favourites of mine are tomatoes, mushrooms, peppers or courgettes. A creamy dressing, especially one based on yoghurt which is lighter than mayonnaise, is a good choice as it adds a necessary richness to counteract the floury quality of the pulses and pasta. Alternatively, try Herb Vinaigrette dressing (page 177) with plenty of fresh herbs to brighten the colour of the salad. Serve pasta salad at room temperature; if it is too cold, you will not appreciate the flavour.

SERVES 4

4oz (110g) chick peas, soaked overnight
8oz (225g) wholewheat pasta
1 tablespoon olive oil
salt
4 sticks of celery, trimmed and diced
3 spring onions, trimmed and diced
1 small head of radicchio, separated
Yoghurt Dressing (page 180)

Drain the chick peas and rinse well. Place in a pan with plenty of fresh water. Bring to the boil and boil fiercely for 10 minutes, then cover and simmer for 30–40 minutes or until quite soft all the way through. Alternatively, cook the chick peas in a pressure cooker for about 20 minutes. Drain well and leave to cool.

To cook the pasta, bring a large pan of water to the boil, add a little oil and salt, then add the pasta. Cook for about 8–10 minutes or until just tender. Drain well, then toss in a little olive oil to prevent the pasta sticking as it cools.

Prepare and toss the remaining salad ingredients and dressing together in a salad bowl. Add the peas and pasta and mix well. Serve at room temperature.

BUTTER BEAN SALAD

Beans look attractive in salads, add extra protein and require little preparation. These satisfying salads are good to use on their own with bread, a savoury muffin or a baked potato as a light snack or supper. Alternatively, serve them as a side dish with a hot light main course such as Toasted Nut Burgers (page 63), Bulgar Wheat Pilaf (page 91) or vegetable-filled pancakes. This salad is best made in advance. Always give the beans a chance to marinate in the dressing to soak up the flavour.

SERVES 4

8oz (225g) dried butter beans, soaked overnight
2 tablespoons olive oil
1 tablespoon white wine vinegar
2 teaspoons chopped fresh tarragon
½ teaspoon celery seeds
1 clove garlic, crushed
salt and pepper
8oz (225g) button mushrooms, wiped and sliced
3oz (75g) green olives, stoned and halved
3oz (75g) gherkins, thickly sliced

Drain the beans and rinse well. Place in a pan with plenty of fresh water. Bring to the boil and boil fiercely for 10 minutes, then simmer for 35–40 minutes or until soft. Drain well.

Shake the oil, vinegar, tarragon, celery seeds and garlic together in a small screw-top jar. Season well. Pour this mixture over the beans immediately they are cooked, then leave to cool. Toss the beans occasionally during cooling to coat well.

Toss all the remaining ingredients into the bean mixture. Serve at room temperature.

THAI FRUIT SALAD

Photograph on page 173

This recipe is a version of one taught by Chalie Amatyakul of the Oriental Cookery School, Bangkok. This sweet and salty lime juice dressing is very popular in the Thai cuisine. You can vary the fruits according to availability, but choose a good mixture of textures and colours.

SERVES 2–4
4oz (110g) mixed purple and green grapes, halved and deseeded
1 medium apple, cored and very thinly sliced
1 large orange, peeled and segmented
4oz (110g) lychees, peeled and stoned
1 teaspoon salt
1 teaspoon brown sugar
juice of 2 limes
groundnut oil for frying
2 tablespoons thinly sliced garlic cloves
2 tablespoons thinly sliced shallots
2 tablespoons peanuts, chopped

Mix all the fruit together in a bowl. Dissolve the salt and sugar in the lime juice in a small bowl. Mix into the fruit and chill.

Meanwhile heat 1–2 inches (2.5–5cm) oil in a medium pan. When hot (test by frying one piece of shallot, and if it bubbles straight away the temperature is right), deep fry the garlic, shallots and peanuts until crisp. Drain well on kitchen paper.

Toss half the deep fried pieces into the fruit. Use the remaining pieces to garnish the salad just before serving.

MANGETOUT AND SESAME SALAD

Photograph on page 173

Mangetout is good in salads with its vibrant colour and crunchy texture. This mixture of fennel, carrot and yellow pepper looks appealing and will brighten up any meal. When making salads with mangetout, steam them very lightly so they retain their colour but soften slightly.

SERVES 4
8oz (225g) mangetout, trimmed
8oz (225g) carrots, peeled
8oz (225g) fennel, trimmed
1 yellow pepper, deseeded
4 spring onions, trimmed and diced
Crunchy Oriental Dressing (page 180)

Steam the mange-tout for 3–4 minutes until slightly softened. Leave to cool. Meanwhile, slice the carrot, fennel and yellow pepper into julienne strips. Mix with the mangetout and spring onions. Toss the dressing into the salad and serve immediately.

FRESH HERB SALAD

This is a different salad from usual as it consists almost entirely of fresh herbs. It makes a colourful addition to a collection of salads or could be served with a hot casserole as an instant tasty garnish. Use this salad to accompany quiches with fillings of beans or lentils as the pungent flavours create a good contrast.

SERVES 4
Dressing
3 tablespoons olive oil
2 teaspoons prepared mustard with herbs or horseradish
1 clove garlic, crushed
2 tablespoons wine vinegar
1 teaspoon clear honey
pepper
Salad
4oz (110g) fresh parsley, finely chopped
4oz (110g) fresh coriander, finely chopped
4oz (110g) sesame seeds, lightly crushed
6 spring onions, trimmed and diced

For the dressing, mix the olive oil, mustard, garlic, vinegar and honey together in a screw-top jar. Shake well, then season with pepper.

For the salad, mix the herbs with the sesame seeds and spring onions. Coat the salad in the dressing, then leave for at least 30 minutes so that the flavours are absorbed.

RICE SALAD WITH FRUIT AND NUTS

Rice is a versatile ingredient to use in salads as it combines well with both savoury and sweet flavours, and many varieties of fruits, nuts and vegetables. For a change of taste you could substitute Cottage Cheese Dressing (page 179). We are rather conditioned to serving fruits as part of a pudding course but they are extremely refreshing in salads. Exotic fruits are an easy way to add a sophisticated touch to a recipe. Peaches, pineapple, nectarine, pawpaw and melon all work very well in rice salads. Poppy seeds, often relegated to garnishing, can be used to add an interesting colour and texture to the rice. Buy them from a delicatessen or wholefood shop where they tend to be cheaper, choosing the blue variety. Poppy seeds keep for several months in a screw-top jar. Serve the salad in the melon halves for a special look as part of a buffet spread.

SERVES 6–8
7oz (200g) or 1 cup long grain brown rice
Dressing
2 tablespoons olive oil
1 tablespoon cider vinegar
1 tablespoon concentrated apple juice
½ teaspoon clear honey
½ teaspoon coriander seeds, crushed
1 teaspoon cumin powder
salt and pepper
Salad
1 melon, halved
2 nectarines, thinly sliced
2oz (50g) Brazil nuts, chopped
2 tablespoons poppy seeds

For the rice, measure the amount into a cup, then bring twice the volume of water to the boil. Add the rice, stir once or twice, bring back to the boil, cover and simmer for 20–25 minutes until the grains are soft and all the water has been absorbed. Drain the rice if necessary and leave to cool.

For the dressing, mix the ingredients together in a screw-top jar and shake well. Adjust seasoning. Pour the dressing over the rice and toss well.

For the salad, discard the melon seeds, then scoop the flesh into balls. Toss the melon, nectarine, nuts and poppy seeds into the rice. Serve at room temperature.

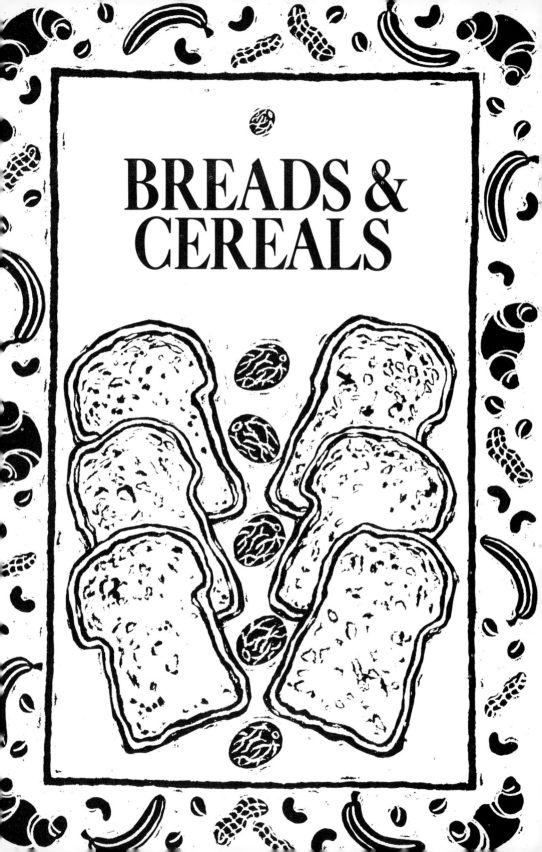

BREADS & CEREALS

Breads and cereals from unrefined grains are a useful part of the diet, making a snack more filling or giving a good start to the day with a wholesome breakfast. Breads can accompany soups, casseroles, salads or pâtés to make a small meal more substantial.

Bread making is not difficult, but it does require a little practice in judging the consistency of the dough. It should be pliable, elastic and fairly soft, but not sticky. It should on no account be dry, or the end result will be dense, hard and disappointing. It is worth trying a few different brands of wholewheat flour until you find one that works well and has the flavour you like. American and Canadian wheats tend to have a higher gluten content which helps with the elasticity of the dough and should enable it to rise well. More experienced bread makers can use British wheats – I especially like the organic varieties available. I suggest you avoid flours that are very coarsely milled if you are new to bread making.

Start with recipes for basic wholewheat breads so you can get used to the technique and the feel of the dough. There is often helpful information on the back of packets of flour, and there is an introduction to the essential ingredients in my earlier book *Vegetarian Kitchen*. However, here I have concentrated on breads using a wider range of flours and cereals – rye, corn and oats – as well as using other ingredients such as nuts, seeds, cheese, different sweetening agents and liquids, all of which keep bread making from becoming repetitive.

The batter method for bread making is explained in the recipe for Seven Seed Bread (opposite). It is a particularly useful technique when working with low gluten flours, or when you want to add a number of different ingredients.

Bread freezes very well, so it is always a good idea to bake a large batch at a time. For best results bake the dough in 1lb (450g) loaf tins, or as rolls or plaits. It is harder to judge whether a 2lb (900g) loaf is cooked thoroughly, and if you are not experienced at kneading, a hole sometimes develops in the centre, which is most disappointing although it doesn't spoil the flavour.

I have included three recipes for cereal grains in this chapter. Although we tend to think of them only as breakfast foods, they do make good snacks at lunch or supper time. The Special Muesli or the Wheatberry Cream could also be used as a pudding served with extra fruit or yoghurt. Use the Malted Roasted Cereal as a topping for crumble, fruit fool or poached fruit. Apart from these cereals, you can use a number of flakes such as oats, rye and barley for porridge.

SEVEN SEED BREAD

Photograph on page 174

Experiment with a basic bread dough by adding different ingredients to the wholewheat flour. When doing this, remember you are reducing the level of gluten in the overall mix, therefore, the dough may take longer to develop. A recipe including low gluten ingredients is best made by the batter method. Make the yeast ferment as you would do normally, but then add all the liquid. Once this mixture has fermented slightly, add about a third or half of the wholewheat flour, mixing in to make a thick smooth batter. The more you beat it, the better it will be. This batter can be left for some time allowing the gluten plenty of time to develop. The other ingredients can then be mixed in.

MAKES 3 × 1LB (450G) LOAVES
1oz (25g) fresh yeast
1 tablespoon molasses
1 tablespoon clear honey
1 pint (570ml) warm water
1lb 6oz (625g) wholewheat flour
1 teaspoon salt
2oz (50g) rye flour
2oz (50g) barley flour or flakes
2oz (50g) oat flakes
1oz (25g) wheatgerm
1oz (25g) sunflower seeds
1 tablespoon linseeds
1 tablespoon sesame seeds
2 tablespoons soya flour

Mix the yeast with the molasses, honey and ¼ pint (150ml) of the warm water in a bowl and leave for 5 minutes until the yeast begins to activate. Add the remaining water and whisk well. Add between a third and a half of the wholewheat flour to make a thin batter. Beat until smooth. Cover the batter and leave in a warm place for at least 15 minutes until a good froth appears on the top.

Mix the remaining ingredients with the remaining flour in a bowl.

Mix all the dry ingredients into the yeast batter and draw up to a rough dough. Knead thoroughly for about 10 minutes until the dough is smooth and elastic. Place the dough in a clean bowl, cover with a damp cloth or cling film and leave for 1 hour or until doubled in size.

Knock back the dough and divide into 3 pieces. Knead each piece

briefly before shaping it into a loaf. Put in 1lb (450g) greased loaf tins and leave to rise for 30–45 minutes.

Preheat the oven to Gas Mark 7, 425°F (220°C). Bake for 30–35 minutes. Once cooked the loaves should turn out easily and sound hollow when tapped on the base. Cool on wire racks.

MALTED OATEN RYE BREAD

Malt extract adds a wonderful flavour to bread, as does pure malt flour, though that is harder to buy. However, malted wholewheat flours are readily available, characterised by the crunchy grains mixed with the flour. A little rye flour and oatflakes are also used in this recipe, and the resulting flavour is quite sweet.

MAKES 1 LARGE COB OR 1LB (450G) LOAF AND 3 SMALL ROLLS

¾oz (20g) fresh yeast
1–2 tablespoons malt extract
½ pint (275ml) warm milk
12oz (350g) malted wholewheat flour
2oz (50g) rye flour
2oz (50g) oatflakes
½ teaspoon salt
extra warm milk

Mix the yeast with the malt extract and ¼ pint (150ml) of the warm milk in a bowl. Leave in a warm place for 5 minutes for the yeast to develop and become frothy.

Mix the flours, oatflakes and salt together in a large bowl. Pour over the yeast ferment and add the remaining warm milk. Mix in well, adding a little extra milk if the dough seems dry as you draw it together. Knead the dough very thoroughly. Transfer to a clean bowl and cover with a damp cloth. Leave the bowl in a warm place for up to 1 hour so that the dough rests and has a chance to rise.

Knock back the dough and knead again briefly. Shape into 1 large cob or make a 1lb (450g) loaf and 3 small rolls. Place in a greased tin or on greased baking sheets. Leave to prove for 30 minutes in a warm place.

Preheat the oven to Gas Mark 7, 425°F (220°C). Bake for 35–40 minutes for the loaf and 15 minutes for the rolls. Turn out and cool on a wire rack.

RYE BREAD WITH CHEESE AND BEER

This sounds like an all-inclusive lunch. It is a good recipe for a savoury loaf with the sharp flavour of the beer complementing the tang of the rye flour. As rye flour is low in gluten, bread made with it does not rise as much as a plain wholewheat loaf, because wheat flour contains so much more gluten. However a small amount of rye flour in a recipe gives a better flavour, and the soya flour and beer will help the rise. This bread is particularly good toasted as the flavour of the cheese is brought out.

MAKES 1 × 2LB (900G) LOAF OR 2 × 1LB (450G) LOAVES

¾oz (20g) fresh yeast
1 tablespoon dark brown muscovado sugar
¼ pint (150ml) warm water
1oz (25g) soya flour
10oz (275g) wholewheat flour
¼ pint (150ml) beer
6oz (175g) rye flour
½ teaspoon salt
4oz (110g) Cheddar cheese, grated

Mix the yeast with the sugar and dissolve it in the warm water in a large bowl. Leave for 5 minutes in a warm place for the yeast to develop and become frothy.

Add the soya flour, half the wholewheat flour and the beer, and beat together thoroughly to make a smooth batter. Cover and leave to rest in a warm place for 30 minutes.

Stir in the remaining wholewheat flour, the rye flour and salt. Draw the ingredients together to form a dough and knead thoroughly. Place the dough in a clean bowl, cover with a damp cloth and leave for 1 hour.

Knead again and sprinkle over the grated cheese. Work the cheese into the dough. Shape into 1 large loaf or 2 smaller ones which you may find easier to handle. Place in a greased 2lb (900g) loaf tin or 2 × 1lb (450g) loaf tins and leave to prove for 30 minutes.

Preheat the oven to Gas Mark 7, 425°F (220°C). Bake for 30–40 minutes. Cool on a wire rack.

BRIOCHE BUNS

Photograph on page 174

It is well worth spending time making this delicious dough as its light yet rich consistency is positively addictive! Although usually made with white flour, it is possible to get a good rise with a wholewheat dough as long as you beat the mixture very thoroughly at all the stages mentioned. Leave the dough to rise for a long time too, so that it can develop properly. If you leave the dough to rise overnight it can be finished quickly for a brunch party or breakfast. If you want to make brioches as part of a savoury meal, remove the tops and scoop out a little of the inside. Fill the brioches with a cheese mixture, such as the Roquefort filling suggested for savoury eclairs (page 150). Stir-fried vegetable mixtures could also be used or a moist filling such as ratatouille or the Steamed Courgettes on page 164, but chopped finely.

MAKES 4
½oz (15g) fresh yeast
1 teaspoon clear honey
3 tablespoons warm water
4 tablespoons warm milk
8oz (225g) wholewheat flour
2oz (50g) sunflower margarine, melted
2 eggs
pinch of salt
4 tablespoons soya flour
beaten egg to glaze

Whisk the yeast, honey and water together in a bowl. Add the milk and 3oz (75g) of the flour. Beat well, then leave for 10 minutes.

Add the melted margarine and beat again thoroughly. Add the beaten eggs, one at a time, then the remaining flour and salt. Beat for at least 10 minutes. Transfer the dough to a large greased bowl and leave in a warm place for 2 hours, or cover and leave overnight in the refrigerator.

Knock back and knead the dough again. Divide into 4 pieces, reserving 2oz (50g) dough for the top.

Place each piece of dough into a greased brioche mould. Make a small indentation in the top and mould the remaining dough into four ½oz (15g) rounds, placing one on top of each brioche. Leave to prove for 20 minutes in a warm place.

Preheat the oven to Gas Mark 7, 425°F (220°C). Brush the brioche buns with beaten egg. Bake for 20–25 minutes. Cool on a wire rack.

RICE BREAD WITH SESAME SEEDS AND HONEY

Adding cooked grain to bread dough is a good way of using up any left overs you have, however small. You can add up to a third of the total weight of the dough again in cooked grains. These will change the texture and consistency of the finished loaf, making it chewier and more moist. This type of loaf keeps very well and is delicious toasted. Other grains, apart from rice, are suitable, particularly cooked wheat and barley, or rye grain, although it is more difficult to buy. This recipe is quite sweet with its delicious mixture of honey and sesame seeds. For a savoury version, use less sweetening and add herbs, finely chopped onion or crushed garlic. The times for rising and baking will be the same.

MAKES 1LB (450G) LOAF AND 4–5 ROLLS

¾oz (20g) fresh yeast
1 tablespoon clear honey
½ pint (275ml) warm water
1 tablespoon soya flour
12oz (350g) wholewheat flour
4oz (110g) cooked brown rice
3 tablespoons sesame seeds, lightly crushed
½ teaspoon salt
extra water if necessary

Dissolve the yeast with the honey in ¼ pint (150ml) warm water in a bowl. Whisk in the soya flour. Leave in a warm place for 5 minutes until frothy.

Put all the remaining ingredients into a large bowl and mix thoroughly. Pour over the yeast ferment and add the rest of the water. Draw the ingredients together to make a soft dough, adding more water if necessary: dough is best moister rather than dry. Knead the dough well, then place in a clean bowl and cover with a damp cloth. Leave to rise for up to 1 hour.

Knock back the dough. Knead again and shape into 1 loaf and 4–5 rolls. Place in a greased 1lb (450g) loaf tin and the rolls on a greased baking tray. Leave to prove for 20–30 minutes in a warm place.

Preheat the oven to Gas Mark 7, 425°F (220°C). Bake for 30–35 minutes for the loaf and 20 minutes for rolls. Cool on a wire rack.

SPECIAL MUESLI

The original concept of muesli was a dish containing a little grain, usually oatflakes, with a high proportion of fruit, particularly grated apple, with lemon, honey and cream or yoghurt. It is light yet very sustaining. Part of the success lies in soaking the oatflakes, then they become extremely creamy and very digestible.

MAKES 1 GENEROUS OR 2 SMALLER SERVINGS

4 tablespoons rolled oats or
2 tablespoons oats and 2 tablespoons granola
4 tablespoons water
1 teaspoon concentrated apple juice
2 teaspoons grated orange rind
1 banana
1oz (25g) raisins
2 tablespoons natural yoghurt
1 tablespoon single cream
2 teaspoons lemon juice
1 teaspoon clear honey
Decoration
3–4 strawberries, sliced

Soak the oats or oat and granola mixture in the water. Stir in the apple juice and orange rind. Leave the mixture to stand overnight.

The next day, thickly slice the banana and mix into the muesli with the remaining ingredients. Spoon into serving dishes and decorate with slices of strawberry.

WHEATBERRY CREAM

This recipe uses wholewheat grain also known as wheatberries which, when cooked, have a delicious springy quality. A traditional British breakfast dish called frumenty is made from this grain; it is plain boiled, then sweetened with raisins and honey. Although good to eat, it is quite demanding on the jaws as the individual wheatberries are hard to break down. I like to add an egg custard to the grains, introducing a creamy caramel flavour and making the dish less intense. It is good hot but also tasty cold. You can vary the type of dried fruit used, but don't add it until near the end or the egg custard will curdle.

SERVES 3–4
4oz (110g) wheatgrain
2 eggs
¼ pint (150ml) skimmed milk
2oz (50g) dates, chopped
½–1oz (15–25g) stem ginger, chopped

Rinse the wheatgrain. Put in a pan with plenty of fresh water. Bring to the boil and simmer for 50–60 minutes until cooked; the wheat will be chewy and some grains will burst open. Drain and leave to cool.

Beat the eggs and milk together in a bowl. Mix in the cooked grain. Transfer to a small pan and cook for 5–10 minutes over a gentle heat until the custard thickens. Add the dates and ginger and cook for a further 1 minute. Serve immediately.

MALTED ROASTED CEREAL

This easy way to prepare crisp cereal, sometimes called granola in the United States, makes a mouthwatering contrast to plain flakes. This recipe can also be used as the basis of a sweet crumble topping.

SERVES 4
6oz (175g) muesli base or mixed jumbo flakes
1oz (25g) sunflower seeds
1oz (25g) peanuts, coarsely chopped
1oz (25g) cashews, coarsely chopped
1–2 tablespoons malt extract
1 tablespoon water
1 tablespoon sunflower oil
grated nutmeg
6 drops of vanilla essence
4oz (110g) sultanas

Preheat the oven to Gas Mark 4, 350°F (180°C). Mix the muesli base with the seeds and nuts in a large bowl. Whisk the malt extract, water and oil together in a small bowl, until fairly well blended. Stir into the muesli base and nuts. Add the nutmeg and vanilla essence.

Spread out the mixture on to shallow baking trays. Roast for about 30 minutes, turning the mixture over once or twice during cooking so that it browns evenly. Leave to cool, then stir in the sultanas.

SESAME BREAD STICKS

Photograph on page 34

Bread sticks are extremely easy to make once you have mastered the technique of rolling them out. The dough should be fairly moist and needs to be lightly kneaded before you start shaping. These breadsticks are made with a mixture enriched with milk, soya flour and ground sesame seeds. It is light and tasty, but also stays soft inside, providing a good contrast to the crisp crust. Generously coat the breadsticks with sesame seeds.

MAKES 16
2oz (50g) sesame seeds
½oz (15g) fresh yeast
1 tablespoon clear honey
6fl oz (175ml) warm milk
6fl oz (175ml) warm water
1lb (450g) wholewheat flour
½ teaspoon salt
1 tablespoon soya flour
Coating
1 egg, beaten

Preheat the oven to Gas Mark 6, 400°F (200°C). Toast all the sesame seeds for 5 minutes in the oven. Grind half of them finely and reserve the remainder for the coating.

Cream the yeast and honey together. Mix the milk and water. Pour ¼ pint (150ml) over the yeast and leave in a warm place for 5 minutes.

Mix the flour, salt, soya flour and ground sesame seeds in a large bowl. Pour over the yeast mixture and the remaining liquid. Work to a dough and knead well. Place in a clean bowl, cover with cling film or a damp cloth and leave in a warm place for 30 minutes.

Knead the dough again briefly. Divide into sixteen pieces and roll out each to a long thin pencil. Brush with beaten egg and roll in the reserved sesame seeds. Place the sticks on greased baking sheets.

Increase the oven temperature to Gas Mark 7, 425°F (220°C). Bake for 10–15 minutes. Cool on a wire rack.

CAKES &
BISCUITS

Strict vegetarians can't eat many commercial cakes and biscuits because of their use of animal fats. Some leading manufacturers are removing this ingredient, a trend which, I hope, will be followed by many more. The other reason for avoiding these products is their low nutritional value. Many are low in fibre and made from high sugar and high fat mixtures with unnecessary flavourings and additives. I think it is safer and better to make your own. I have experimented a great deal with unrefined ingredients, low fat recipes and sugar substitutes, trying to make tempting but healthy cakes and biscuits.

By taking the small step of using wholewheat flour in cakes, you will immediately boost the fibre and nutrient content. There are plenty of flours to choose from; a fine milled variety will be lightest and organically grown English wheat flours have a delicious flavour. Brown rice flour could also be used as a replacement for some of the wheat flour, giving an even lighter texture, but a slightly more crumbly crumb. A wholewheat cake will never be identical in look or flavour to one made of refined ingredients but it certainly needn't be dull or heavy. The denser texture is more filling so you usually end up eating smaller portions.

Converting cake recipes to be low in sugar or to use no added sugar is relatively easy. First start by cutting down the standard amount of sugar used until you find an acceptable minimum level of sweetness. It is surprising how this keeps changing as one's sweet tooth diminishes. However a complete lack of sugar can make a cake dry and tasteless. Solve this problem by using cooked dried fruit purées, sugar-free jams and concentrated fruit juice as sugar substitutes, they add a pleasant sweetness and good fruity flavour. Dates are particularly useful as they are roughly 66% natural sugar and so obviously add the most sweetness. There is a difference between obtaining sugar in this way rather than from sucrose. The natural sugars present in fruit are easier for the body to metabolise. Fruit sugars have other nutrients too, so although dates, for example, are two-thirds sugar, the remaining third is fibre and valuable vitamins and minerals. Sucrose, or ordinary sugar as we know it, contains no nutrients whatsoever.

Finding low fat and fat free recipes is not so easy and the end result is often dry or tough. If you are going to use a fat, at least choose a good quality oil rather than a saturated hardened margarine or butter. A successful recipe using this idea is the Apple and Pecan Cake. Another way of solving the high fat problem is to make a different type of cake altogether. American-style muffins are a cross between a quick bread and a cake. These mixtures use a little oil enriched with skimmed milk and eggs. First the dry ingredients are put together, then the liquids are

mixed separately, and finally everything is combined. One good fat free recipe is the sponge, used for trifle, on page 218. It works very well, even with wholewheat flour.

Fillings and toppings
There are a number of different toppings and fillings to make that are good tasty alternatives to high fat butter creams or high sugar icings.

Purées of cooked dried fruits, especially dates and apricots, make very good fillings. These can be lightened and flavoured with fresh fruit, such as banana or pineapple. Purée in the fresh fruit once the dried fruit mixture has cooled. For a richer filling, add a little tahini, crème fraîche or thick natural yoghurt. For extra texture use chopped nuts.

For toppings, carob icing (page 209) is popular for biscuits as well as cakes. Alternatively, use a sugar-free jam boiled up with some water and lemon juice to make a glaze. Spread this over the cake, then sprinkle on nuts, seeds or coconut flakes to make an interesting finish.

DIGESTIVE BISCUITS

These make excellent low-sugar, nutty, digestive style biscuits. They are simple to make and will keep for several days in an airtight jar, or you could make enough to freeze a batch. I have also made a version without any sugar at all, which I found just as successful.

MAKES 12 LARGE BISCUITS
4oz (110g) wholewheat flour
pinch of salt
2oz (50g) sunflower margarine
1 tablespoon skimmed milk powder
1 tablespoon soft brown sugar
1 tablespoon wheatgerm
2–3 tablespoons water

Preheat the oven to Gas Mark 5, 375°F (190°C). Mix the flour and salt in a large bowl. Rub in the margarine until the mixture resembles fine breadcrumbs. Add the remaining ingredients, except the water, and rub in lightly. Add enough of the water to make a soft, rather wet dough.

Roll out the dough fairly thinly. Cut into 12 rounds, place on lightly greased baking sheets. Bake for 15–20 minutes. Cool on wire racks.

GREG'S CANADIAN BRAN MUFFINS

These are delicious both at breakfast or for afternoon tea. As they keep well, certainly for 2–3 days, you can make these muffins ahead of time. The raisins provide a pleasant sweetness, while bran gives a fairly coarse texture and fibre. Remember though, when using bran, that it's rather like blotting paper with its capacity to absorb liquid. So make the recipe quite moist. Once the mixture is made, it should be baked immediately or the muffins will not rise well.

MAKES 10–12
3oz (75g) bran
¾oz (20g) wheatgerm
3oz (75g) wholewheat flour
1 teaspoon bicarbonate of soda
pinch of salt
1 teaspoon ground cinnamon
3oz (75g) raisins
2 eggs, beaten
2 tablespoons clear honey
2 tablespoons molasses
½ pint (275ml) skimmed milk

Preheat the oven to Gas Mark 6, 400°F (200°C). Mix the bran, wheatgerm, flour, soda, salt and cinnamon together in a large bowl. Add the raisins and mix in well.

Beat the eggs very thoroughly in a jug to make the final result lighter. Add the honey, molasses and milk and beat well again. Pour this mixture over the dry ingredients and mix to a thick batter.

Spoon the batter into well greased deep bun tins or muffin tins. Bake immediately for 20–25 minutes. Leave in the tin for 2–3 minutes, then turn out and cool on a wire rack.

GINGER MUFFINS

These light buns have a spicy, fruit flavour and pale golden colour. They are delicious eaten freshly made, still warm, but they will keep for one or two days. Purée the apricots using a food processor or blender as the lighter the purée, the better the texture of the cooked muffin.

MAKES 12

2oz (50g) apricots, soaked in 1 pint (570ml) boiling water
2 eggs
1oz (25g) demerara sugar
1oz (25g) clear honey
2 tablespoons sunflower oil
8oz (225g) wholewheat flour
8oz (225g) medium oatmeal
2–3 teaspoons ground ginger
2½ teaspoons baking powder
pinch of salt

Place the apricots with their soaking water in a pan, cover and cook for 35–40 minutes until tender. Drain, reserving the liquid, and purée the fruit in a blender or food processor.

Preheat the oven to Gas Mark 6, 400°F (200°C). Beat the eggs thoroughly in a bowl and add the sugar, honey and oil. Blend into the apricot purée in the blender or food processor.

Mix the flour with the oatmeal, ginger, baking powder and salt in a separate bowl. Stir the purée mixture into the dry ingredients.

Spoon immediately into greased bun tins or muffin tins. Bake for 18–20 minutes or until well risen.

SAVOURY OATCAKES

These traditional sugar-free savoury oatcakes are simple to make and yet so versatile. Their dry texture makes them a good accompaniment to soups and casseroles, or they can be spread with a pâté or even a sweet topping. The texture is quite crumbly so handle them carefully.

MAKES 24

12oz (350g) fine or medium oatmeal
4oz (110g) wholewheat flour
1 teaspoon baking powder
½ teaspoon bicarbonate of soda
1 teaspoon salt
4oz (110g) solid vegetable fat or butter
5–6 tablespoons cold water

Preheat the oven to Gas Mark 6, 400°F (200°C). Put the oatmeal and flour in a large bowl and mix in the baking powder, bicarbonate of soda and salt thoroughly. Rub in the fat until the mixture resembles breadcrumbs. Add enough water to make a soft, moist dough and knead slightly.

Divide the mixture into 6 pieces. Roll out each one into a circle and mark into 4 sections, or roll out the dough and cut into rounds.

Place the oatcakes on a baking tray. Bake for 15–20 minutes. Cool on a wire rack.

MINIATURE CASHEW SCONES

Photograph on page 33

These light, nutty scones are quick to make and transform a soup into more of a meal. If the soup is fairly substantial, I think a miniature scone is more appetising than a chunk of bread. This versatile recipe could also be used as a cocktail snack or party appetiser, topped with spreads.

MAKES 16
2½oz (60g) cashew nuts
7oz (200g) wholewheat flour
½ teaspoon salt
3 teaspoons baking powder
2 tablespoons soya flour
2oz (50g) sunflower margarine
about 6fl oz (175ml) milk
1 egg, lightly beaten

Preheat the oven to Gas Mark 6, 400°F (200°C). Toast the cashew nuts in the oven for 5 minutes or until lightly browned. Reserve 2 tablespoons, then finely grind the remaining nuts in a nut mill or coffee grinder.

Mix the flour, salt, baking powder and soya flour together in a bowl. Add the ground nuts. Rub in the margarine until the mixture looks like fine breadcrumbs. Add the milk and mix to a soft dough.

Quickly pat out the dough to ½ inch (1cm) thick. Cut into sixteen 1½ inch (3.5cm) rounds. Place the scones on a greased baking sheet and brush with beaten egg. Roughly chop the remaining cashew nuts and sprinkle on top.

Increase the oven temperature to Gas Mark 7, 425°F (220°C). Bake for 10–15 minutes. Cool on a wire rack.

APPLE AND PECAN CAKE

This is a useful cake recipe designed for apples, although other fruit such as pears or apricots could be used, and other nuts too, such as almonds, hazels and walnuts. It is easily made too as the method is based on the American way of mixing wet and dry ingredients, so there is no creaming or rubbing in to be done. Oil gives cakes a good light texture, they cut and keep well. It is important to whisk the oil and honey very well together, not only to blend them but so that as much air as possible is beaten in. This greatly improves the end result. Keep the apples, or indeed other fruits you use, chunky so that they provide a good contrast of texture to the cake itself. This is good not only at tea time but as a pudding after a light main course.

MAKES 8 INCH (20CM) CAKE

4oz (110g) sultanas
juice of 1 orange
2 tablespoons brandy
2 teaspoons grated orange rind
½ pint (275ml) sunflower oil
¼ pint (150ml) clear honey
2 eggs, beaten
8oz (225g) wholewheat flour
2 teaspoons ground cinnamon
1 teaspoon bicarbonate of soda
½ teaspoon salt
3oz (75g) pecan nuts, roughly chopped
2 medium cooking apples, peeled, cored and chopped

Soak the sultanas in the orange juice and brandy. Stir in the orange rind and leave for at least 30 minutes. Purée in the blender or food processor to make a chunky sweet sauce.

Preheat the oven to Gas Mark 2, 300°F (160°C). Whisk the oil and honey together until well blended. It is best to do this using an electric whisk as so much more air can be incorporated, making the cake very light. Beat in the eggs thoroughly, one at a time, then beat in the sultana purée. Mix the flour, cinnamon, bicarbonate of soda and salt together. Add to the oil mixture and stir in well. Finally, mix in the pecan nuts and apple pieces.

Spoon the mixture into a greased and lined 8 inch (20cm) cake tin. Bake for 1¼–1½ hours or until a skewer inserted in the centre comes out clean. Leave the cake in the tin for 15 minutes to cool before turning out.

BANANA AND SUNFLOWER CAKE

This cake is based on the creaming method but uses a dried fruit purée as a sweetening agent, and mashed banana and sunflower seeds for extra flavour and texture. The end result is delicious, the texture is quite dense and moist and rather pudding-like. You can either serve the cake plain, or sandwich with a cream filling and spread over a topping for an attractive look for a special tea party. Mashed banana with orange or lemon juice works well, or try a mixture of apricot purée and crème fraîche.

MAKES 7 INCH (18CM) CAKE

3oz (75g) dried apricots
4oz (110g) sunflower margarine or butter
2 eggs
4oz (110g) wholewheat flour
1 teaspoon baking powder
1 banana, mashed
2oz (50g) sunflower seeds

Snip the apricots into small pieces. Place in a pan, cover with hot water and simmer for 20–30 minutes or until quite soft. Add a little more water if necessary during cooking and stir the apricots several times as this helps to break them down. Purée the apricots in a blender or food processor to make a soft paste. Leave to cool.

Preheat the oven to Gas Mark 4, 350°F (180°C). Cream the margarine with the apricot purée until light and fluffy. Beat in the eggs thoroughly, one at a time, adding a little flour if the mixture begins to curdle. Sift the flour with the baking powder and beat into the apricot mixture. Add the mashed banana and sunflower seeds.

Spoon the mixture into a greased and floured 7 inch (18cm) cake tin or 1lb (450g) loaf tin. Bake for 35–40 minutes or until a skewer inserted in the centre comes out clean. If cooked in a loaf tin, the cake may take longer. Cool on a wire rack.

Opposite: Kaye's Scotch Cookies (page 210) and Carob and Orange Cake (page 209)
Overleaf: Pineapple Sorbet (page 218) and Ricotta Cheesecake (page 220)

CAROB AND ORANGE CAKE

Photograph on page 207

This is a deliciously moist cake that is extremely easy to make. As with the Apple and Pecan Cake recipe on page 205, it is very important to beat it thoroughly. This cake is quite sweet but, if you prefer, you can increase the sugar to 2oz (50g). It is easy to make variations on this basic recipe. You can use different fruit juices, add spices such as cinnamon or allspice, or essences of vanilla or rum.

MAKES 7 INCH (18CM) CAKE
2oz (50g) dried dates
4fl oz (110ml) sunflower oil
4fl oz (110ml) orange juice
1 tablespoon brown sugar
1 tablespoon malt extract
3 eggs
3oz (75g) wholewheat flour
3oz (75g) brown rice flour
1oz (25g) carob powder
2 teaspoons baking powder
2 teaspoons grated orange rind
Filling
1 ripe banana
1 tablespoon orange juice
1 tablespoon carob powder
Icing
1oz (25g) carob bar
¼oz (7g) butter
1 teaspoon concentrated apple juice
1–2 tablespoons milk
Decoration
extra grated carob bar or chopped nuts

Preheat the oven to Gas Mark 4, 350°F (180°C). For the date purée, chop the dates well and remove any stones. Put them in a small pan, cover with a little hot water and gently simmer for 5–10 minutes, breaking them down with a wooden spoon. Add a little more water if necessary but do not make the paste too thin. Purée or mash well and leave to cool.

Whisk the oil and fruit juice together very thoroughly in a bowl. Add the sugar, malt extract, eggs and cooled date purée. Whisk until frothy.

In a separate bowl, sift the flours, carob powder and baking powder together. Mix half of this mixture into the liquid ingredients. Beat in thoroughly, then add the remainder and the orange rind and beat again. Spoon the mixture into 2 greased and lined 7 inch (18cm) sandwich tins. Bake for 30 minutes. Turn out and cool on a wire rack.

For the filling, mash the banana with the orange juice and carob powder until smooth.

For the icing, melt the carob bar with the butter in a small bowl over hot water, being careful not to overheat. Beat the mixture until smooth. Add the concentrated apple juice and enough milk to make the mixture soft. Leave to cool.

Sandwich the cake together with the filling. Spread the icing over the top, then decorate with extra grated carob or chopped nuts.

KAYE'S SCOTCH COOKIES

Photograph on page 207

Scotch cookies are the name given to shortbread biscuits in Canada. This is a traditional recipe orginally from Scotland but one that emigrated, was rechristened, and has now returned. I have altered the ingredients to include unrefined flour and brown sugar so it may well be closer to the original. Grinding the demerara sugar makes the biscuit much more crunchy.

MAKES 24

6oz (175g) demerara sugar
7oz (200g) wholewheat flour
6oz (175g) cornmeal, finely ground
8oz (225g) butter or sunflower margarine, cut into small pieces

Preheat the oven to Gas Mark 6, 400°F (200°C). Grind the demerara sugar finely in a coffee grinder or blender until the consistency of icing sugar. Put into a large bowl and mix in the flour and cornmeal. Rub in the butter until the mixture resembles fine breadcrumbs, or blend in a food processor. Knead the dough into a smooth ball.

Form the dough into a block and cut off small rectangles, about 1 × 3 inches (2.5 × 7.5cm) and ½ inch (1cm) thick, to make biscuits. Prick all over and place on a greased baking sheet. Bake for 15 minutes or until crisp and fairly well browned. Cool on a wire rack.

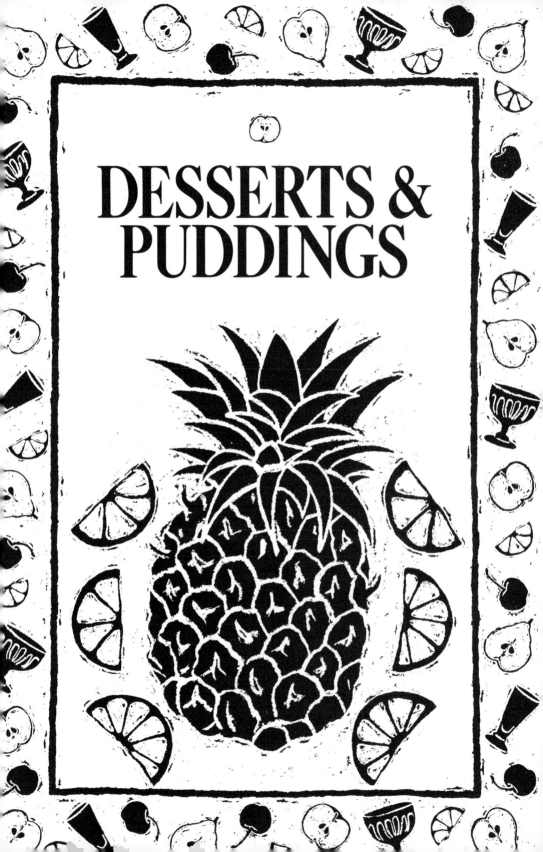

DESSERTS & PUDDINGS

Desserts and puddings do not generally pose much of a problem to vegetarians except with the commercial use of animal fats in pastry, gelatine from animal bones in mousses, cheesecake, yoghurt and jelly, and beef suet for steamed puddings and mincemeat. Luckily vegetarian alternatives are becoming more widely used.

Fresh fruit is an ideal way to end a meal – served on its own, or with yoghurt, cream or crème fraîche as an accompaniment. The fruit bowl can be extended with dried fruit and nuts in shells.

Fruit salads are always delicious and eye-catching. Pick a theme of tropical fruits or a mixture of fruits of varying shades of the same colour. Cut the fruit attractively, occasionally leaving the pieces chunky. Do not drown the fruit in a sugary dressing. Diluted concentrated apple juice makes an excellent base or use other fresh fruit juices with alcohol added for special occasions. Thicker liquid bases can be made from puréed fruit. Bananas work particularly well. Other fruit salads can be created from dried fruit, especially a good mixture of apple rings, figs, apricots, prunes and peaches. They involve little preparation, but be sure to give the fruit plenty of time to soak and add enough liquid, such as water, flavoured fruit teas or fruit juices, to plump them up. For a warming winter dish, stew the fruit gently with mulled wine spices such as cinnamon and nutmeg.

For simple hot puddings, fresh fruit can also be poached or baked and served with a sweet sauce. A fruit purée is a versatile base for a pudding – serve it with pancakes, as crumble fillings, or mixed with custards, creams or yoghurt for fruit fools. I have given a basic crumble recipe; it is a very popular pudding and both the top and filling can be varied in many ways.

I've also given a recipe for confectioner's custard made with unrefined ingredients, skimmed milk and less sugar than usual. Use it to turn a fruit purée into a delicious fool, or to line a cold cooked pastry case – cover it with slices of fresh fruit and a glaze for a wonderful tart. A different type of custard recipe from Thailand is also included.

For pastry style puddings, you need a richer pastry, so I have suggested one using skimmed milk powder and cinnamon. It is filled with mincemeat and apples, but you could try other combinations.

Soft cheeses are increasingly more available and these can be used to make uncomplicated cheesecakes. The Ricotta Cheesecake has a delicate flavour and texture, and sets in the refrigerator. There is also a carob trifle, ideal for special occasions.

RHUBARB AND BANANA CRUMBLE

Always a favourite pudding with me, crumble seems irresistible both hot and cold. This has an excellent low sugar fruit filling which may seem surprising as sharp rhubarb is one of the main ingredients. It is sweetened with a quickly made sultana purée. This type of purée can be used as a basis for a sweet sauce to accompany plain poached fruit dishes or pies, or mixed with other fresh fruits for different fillings. I have made the crumble topping with oil for a crisper texture and also added hazelnuts for extra crunch. Other flakes, flours or mueslis can be used to give different flavours. A crumble topping is a particularly good way to introduce a variety of grains into the diet.

SERVES 4

4oz (110g) sultanas
½ pint (275ml) orange juice
1 ripe banana, sliced
1¼lb (550g) rhubarb, trimmed
1 teaspoon ground allspice
1 tablespoon clear honey
Crumble Topping
2oz (50g) wholewheat flour
2oz (50g) oatflakes
1oz (25g) hazelnuts, roasted
2–3 tablespoons sunflower oil

Place the sultanas and orange juice in a small pan, cover and cook for 15–20 minutes until well plumped up and quite soft. Leave to cool slightly, then purée roughly with the banana in a blender or food processor to form a sauce.

Cut the rhubarb stalks into ½ inch (1cm) pieces and mix into the sauce. Poach the rhubarb for about 10 minutes over a gentle heat or 1 hour in a slow cooker until just soft. Make sure the rhubarb does not disintegrate too much or the texture will be spoilt. Flavour with allspice, then sweeten with honey to taste. Spoon into a ovenproof dish.

For the crumble topping, mix together the flour and oatflakes. Preheat the oven to Gas Mark 5, 375°F (190°C). Place the hazelnuts on a small baking tray, and bake for about 10 minutes until lightly browned. Rub off any loose skins. Coarsely chop the nuts and add to the oat and flour mixture. Rub in the oil so that the ingredients are well coated. Sprinkle the crumble topping on the rhubarb. Bake for 20–25 minutes or until the crumble topping is just browned.

CONFECTIONER'S CUSTARD

This is a version of a classic French crème pâtissière. I make it with skimmed milk and less sugar than most recipes suggest. As it is usually part of a dish with other sweet ingredients, 1oz (25g) sugar is enough. The cream is thickened with brown rice flour which is light and blends in smoothly, giving a very satisfactory result. This custard is easy to make as long as you are patient when heating the mixture as it takes at least 15 minutes for the sauce to thicken. If you rush it, the eggs will curdle and the custard will be ruined. Once made, this custard has a variety of uses. Blend into cooked and puréed fruit such as apples or apricots, then fold in a stiffly beaten egg white to make a delicious mousse. Spread chilled custard over a baked pastry case, cover with fresh fruit, especially summer fruits, and a glaze to make a light flan.

SERVES 4
½ pint (275ml) skimmed milk
1 egg
1 egg yolk
1oz (25g) light soft brown sugar
1oz (25g) fine milled brown rice flour
2–3 drops of vanilla essence

Heat the milk in a heavy pan until it begins to steam. Whisk the eggs and sugar in a bowl until light and fluffy, then whisk in the flour until smooth. Pour on the hot milk, beating well, then return the mixture to the pan. Gently heat the custard for about 15 minutes, stirring constantly, until it thickens and reaches boiling point. Simmer for 2–3 minutes, then add the vanilla essence.

Transfer the mixture to a clean bowl, cover with a piece of lightly buttered greaseproof paper to prevent a skin forming. Leave to cool. Keep refrigerated and use within 24 hours.

APPLE FOOL

This is a simple way to make a delicious light fruit dessert. Ring the changes by using other fruits or spices and enrich the fool with chopped nuts, chopped fresh fruit or whipped cream. Do not just restrict this idea to puddings, it is delicious served as a breakfast dish as well, especially when accompanied with Wheatberry Cream (page 196).

SERVES 4

1 quantity Confectioner's Custard (opposite)
1 teaspoon butter or sunflower margarine
1lb (450g) cooking apples, peeled, cored and finely sliced
1 teaspoon ground cinnamon
1 tablespoon water
1 egg white

Make up the confectioner's custard. Melt the butter in a small pan, add the apples, cinnamon and water. Cover tightly and cook for 5–8 minutes until soft, stirring occasionally and adding a little more water if necessary. Cool slightly, then purée with the confectioner's custard in a blender or food processor until smooth.

Whisk the egg white until stiff in a separate bowl. Fold it carefully into the apple purée. Spoon the mixture into glasses or a serving dish and chill.

THAI COCONUT CUSTARD

This Thai dessert makes a rich smooth dish that is not sickly sweet. The traditional garnish is deep fried shallots, which may seem strange to Western tastes. I find grated fresh coconut or slices of orange are more appealing. This coconut custard could also be baked as a topping over a portion of fresh or cooked fruit, in which case it will serve 6. Alternatively, bake the custard in a shallow tray, leave to cool, then cut into small pieces and serve as a sweetmeat.

SERVES 4

5oz (150g) creamed coconut
5–6fl oz (150–175ml) hot water
1oz (25g) soft brown sugar
2oz (50g) soya flour
2 eggs, beaten

Preheat the oven to Gas Mark 4, 350°F (180°C). Grate the creamed coconut, then blend with the hot water to make a smooth sauce the consistency of double cream. Heat the coconut mixture and sugar in a small pan over a low heat until the sugar has dissolved. Remove the pan from the heat and mix in the soya flour. Add the eggs and beat in thoroughly. Pour the custard into 4 small ovenproof dishes or ramekins, set in a bain-marie. Bake for 20 minutes or until lightly browned.

MINCEMEAT AND APPLE FLAN

Luckily there are now plenty of vegetarian-style mincemeats on the market that do not contain the traditional beef suet. There are also low sugar and no added sugar varieties so mincemeat, or mincefruit as I have seen it described, is becoming a relatively healthy product. Add skimmed milk powder and cinnamon to the shortcrust pastry to give it a good nutty flavour and hint of spice.

SERVES 4–6
Pastry
4oz (110g) wholewheat flour
pinch of salt
1 teaspoon ground cinnamon
2oz (50g) sunflower margarine
½oz (15g) skimmed milk powder
2–3 tablespoons cold water
Filling
12oz (350g) cooking apples, peeled, cored and sliced
4–6oz (110–175g) mincemeat
1 teaspoon ground cinnamon
1–2 teaspoons clear honey
1–2 teaspoons lemon juice

For the pastry, put the flour, salt and cinnamon in a large bowl, then rub in the margarine until the mixture resembles fine breadcrumbs. Mix in the milk powder. Add enough cold water to make a soft dough, moist rather than dry. Wrap the dough in polythene and leave to rest for 30 minutes in a cool place or the refrigerator.

Preheat the oven to Gas Mark 6, 400°F (200°C). Roll out the dough and use to line a 7 inch (18cm) flan ring. Press the pastry into the base and sides well. Prick all over with a fork. Bake blind for 3–4 minutes until just set.

For the filling, arrange a layer of apple slices over the base of the pastry case. Cover with a little mincemeat, dotted over roughly. Warm the cinnamon, honey and lemon juice together and brush over the top. Cover with another layer of apples and mincemeat, then continue the layers until all the filling is used up. Leave enough honey mixture to brush over the top.

Bake for 35–40 minutes or until the apples are well cooked and the pastry shrinks slightly away from the edge of the flan ring. Serve warm with natural yoghurt, smetana or cream.

YOGHURT ICE CREAM

Yoghurt ice creams have a very refreshing flavour and a mild tang.

MAKES 1 PINT (570ML)
1oz (25g) sultanas
1oz (25g) raisins
1oz (25g) dried apricots, cut into slivers
¼ pint (150ml) fruit juice
15fl oz (400ml) natural yoghurt
2oz (50g) pecans, chopped
2–3 teaspoons clear honey

Soak the sultanas, raisins and apricots in the fruit juice for 2–3 hours. Alternatively, simmer for 10 minutes and leave to cool.

Roughly purée the fruit with the juice and natural yoghurt in a blender or food processor. Add the nuts and honey to taste. Place in a freezer-proof container and freeze until firm, stirring several times during freezing. Alternatively, use an ice-cream maker for a very smooth result. Defrost for 10–15 minutes before serving.

BANANA AND CAROB ICE CREAM

SERVES 4
2 bananas
1 tablespoon concentrated apple juice
1 tablespoon clear honey
juice of ½ lemon
¼ pint (150ml) milk
2–3 teaspoons carob powder
½ pint (275ml) whipping cream

Purée the bananas, apple juice, honey and lemon juice in a blender or food processor until smooth. Add the milk and purée again. Add the carob powder to taste and blend in.

Whip the cream in a bowl until stiff, then fold this into the mixture. Adjust the sweetening with honey if necessary. Place in a freezerproof container and freeze until firm, stirring several times during freezing, or use an ice-cream maker. Defrost for 10–15 minutes before serving.

PINEAPPLE SORBET

Photograph on page 208

This extremely refreshing fruit dessert is sweetened by a sultana purée, therefore there is no need to add extra sugar. Other fresh fruits, such as mango or kiwi fruit, could be substituted for the pineapple, but include the banana as it adds a necessary creamy quality.

MAKES 1 PINT (570ML)
4oz (110g) sultanas
½ pint (275ml) orange juice
8oz (225g) fresh pineapple, chopped
2 bananas
juice of 1 lime

For the sultana purée, place the sultanas in a pan with the orange juice, cover and simmer for 30 minutes. Leave to cool completely.

Purée the sultanas with the pineapple and banana until completely smooth. Add the lime juice to taste. Place the mixture in a freezerproof container and freeze until firm, stirring once or twice during freezing. Defrost for about 15–20 minutes before serving.

CAROB RUM TRIFLE

This is a mouthwatering pudding to be enjoyed on special occasions. Trifles are always popular and they look particularly good presented in cut glass bowls. The trifle sponge, a fat-free whisked mixture, is a useful technique to master as it can make the basis of a very good ordinary cake, simply filled and iced. To make the sponge mixture light, thoroughly beat the eggs and sugar mixture and fold in the flour carefully. Use wholewheat flour, but choose a variety that is finely milled so the sponge will be as light as possible. I often make a sponge using pear and apple spread as a sugar substitute and find that it works just as well as conventional recipes using sugar. Trifles can be made with a variety of alcoholic flavourings or fruit juices. It is important to have enough liquid to soak the sponge but not too much to make it soggy. If you want to make a more health-conscious trifle, use quark, curd cheese or tofu as a substitute for custard. Blend until light and add flavour by puréeing in some fresh fruit or cooked dried fruit. The end result, although not like traditional trifle, is delicious.

SERVES 6–8
Sponge
2 eggs
1oz (25g) light brown sugar or *2 tablespoons pear and apple spread*
2oz (50g) wholewheat flour
Trifle
2–3 tablespoons sugar-free blackberry or bilberry jam
2 tablespoons rum or orange liqueur
juice of 2 oranges
2 teaspoons grated orange rind
2 bananas, sliced
Custard
2 eggs
1oz (25g) light brown sugar
¼ pint (150ml) milk
½oz (15g) carob powder
½ pint (275ml) double or whipping cream
Decoration
1oz (25g) carob bar, grated

Preheat the oven to Gas Mark 5, 375°F (190°C). For the sponge, whisk the eggs and sugar or pear and apple spread together in a bowl until thick, light, frothy and a trail is left by the beaters. Sift the flour and carefully fold in, keeping as much of the air in the mixture as possible.

Line the base of a 7 inch (18cm) cake tin with greaseproof paper and spoon in the sponge mixture. Bake for 25 minutes. Remove from the tin and cool on a wire rack.

Once cool, split in half and spread jam in the middle. Sandwich the halves together, then cut into ½ inch (1cm) cubes. Place the sponge cubes in an attractive glass dish. Soak the cubes in the rum and orange juice. Sprinkle over the orange rind.

For the custard, beat the eggs thoroughly with the sugar in a pan. Pour over the milk and whisk in the carob powder. Heat the mixture gently, stirring continuously, until it thickens and coats the back of a spoon. Leave the carob custard to cool.

Beat the cream until thick. Fold half the cream into the cooled custard.

To assemble the trifle, arrange the banana slices thickly over the soaked sponge. Cover with the carob custard, then spread over the remaining cream. Grate a little carob on top to decorate. Alternatively, use grated orange rind.

RICOTTA CHEESECAKE

Photograph on page 208

There is something very indulgent about cheesecakes with their creamy flavour and snowy whiteness. Baked versions are certainly more robust and easier to handle, but I prefer an uncooked version. The problem with most recipes, from a vegetarian point of view, is they require gelatine to make the mixture set. Agar agar is a substitute but it does tend to be rather unpredictable. This recipe relies on a mixture of ricotta cheese and thick yoghurt which, once beaten together and chilled, will set lightly. This cheesecake is delicious but delicate so handle it carefully. Add fruit as a decoration and serve with extra fruit if preferred. I have suggested an oatcake base but a digestive biscuit mixture would do just as well. If you are concerned about the fragility of the cheesecake, use the same mixture in ramekins with or without a base; it should fill 4–6 dishes. Leave to chill, then serve in the dishes decorated with fruit.

MAKES 7 INCH (18CM) CAKE OR 4–6 RAMEKINS

Base
4oz (110g) sunflower margarine or butter
2oz (50g) soft brown sugar or fruit purée
4oz (110g) wholewheat flour
4oz (110g) oatflakes
Topping
10oz (275g) ricotta cheese
8oz (225g) natural yoghurt, strained
1–2 tablespoons clear honey
6 drops of vanilla essence
2 teaspoons lemon juice
1–2 kiwi fruit or 12 strawberries

Preheat the oven to Gas Mark 4, 350°F (180°C). For the base, cream the margarine and sugar or fruit purée together in a bowl until light and fluffy. Mix in the flour and oat flakes, then beat to form a rough dough. Press the mixture, not too thickly, into a 7 inch (18cm) loose based cake tin or spring mould. Any trimmings can be used to make biscuits. Bake for 15–20 minutes or until fairly crisp. Leave the base to cool completely.

For the topping, beat the ricotta, yoghurt and honey together in a bowl until well blended and smooth. Add the vanilla essence and lemon juice to taste, then adjust the sweetening if necessary.

Spoon the topping over the baked base and chill for at least 24 hours until set. Decorate with kiwi fruit slices or strawberries just before serving.

THE
VEGETARIAN
KITCHEN

Τhis chapter contains useful information on large and small pieces of kitchen equipment. There are notes on how to use both the freezer and the microwave, with particular reference to vegetarian foods, what works best and how to defrost. There follows a short section outlining the function of smaller electrical equipment such as food mixers and blenders, which may help you to decide whether an appliance would be a useful addition to your kitchen.

Finally, I have compiled an A-Z of the more unusual ingredients mentioned in this book, about which you may want to know more, as well as notes on the staple ingredients such as pulses and grains.

FREEZERS

Used well, the freezer can save you time, energy and money. Most of the rules that apply to freezing conventional foods apply to vegetarian ingredients. In general, most savoury and sweet dishes can be frozen.

After a certain amount of time, the taste and texture of frozen foods may deteriorate. Length of storage depends on several factors. Here are some guidelines:

🗲 Make sure the quality of the food to be frozen is good. Although freezing is recognised as an excellent method of food preservation, it won't improve the quality of the product – so always choose the best.

🗲 Wrap up food to be frozen very well as exposure to the oxygen in the air will cause deterioration.

🗲 Freeze food as quickly as possible so that only small ice crystals are formed which do not damage the cell structure of the food.

🗲 Fatty foods or dishes with a high fat content should not be frozen for long or the fat may go rancid.

🗲 The flavour of salt becomes stronger when frozen, and its presence also accelerates the rancidity of fatty foods – so be very light handed with the seasoning. Other herbs and spices, particularly garlic, may change in flavour after several months, so do not freeze dishes with these ingredients too long.

What to freeze

Most foods used in a vegetarian or wholefood diet will freeze. Some of the exceptions are hard-boiled eggs, cottage cheese, single cream, mayonnaise and salad ingredients.

Cooked pulses and grains freeze well. Use the open freezing method for these items as this way you can take out the exact amount you need. To open freeze, spread out the food on a large tray or plate, leaving air space around each item if possible. Freeze until solid, then pack in bags or boxes. Pulses and grains will keep for six months.

In general, vegetables freeze well. If you blanch them first, their freezer life is greater as certain enzymes and bacteria that cause deterioration are destroyed. Most vegetables will keep up to one year. Exceptions are onions, which keep only six months, and mushrooms, which should be used within three months. Fruits can also be frozen, though some discolour or collapse on defrosting, so fruit purées may be a better solution.

Nuts will keep frozen for a year in the freezer provided they are not salted. Nut butters also keep well.

Tofu can be frozen, but its consistency changes and it becomes spongy in texture and beige in colour. Once frozen, it is probably best to disguise tofu in a casserole or mashed into a filling. Thawed frozen tofu absorbs more liquid.

Most savoury vegetarian dishes can be frozen either cooked or uncooked. If they are frozen cooked, it is best to undercook them slightly initially so that they retain a good texture when reheated. Also bear in mind that dishes with a high fat content do not keep so long. Certain sauces separate on defrosting; this does not affect the taste but the appearance is spoilt. This can be remedied by brisk beating or a quick whizz in the blender. Breads and pastries can be frozen for three to six months.

Defrosting

The microwave oven has made a huge difference in this respect and there is advice on page 225 about using a microwave for defrosting.

If you are thawing food to reheat it by conventional methods, then leave overnight in the refrigerator to ensure it is thoroughly defrosted before reheating. A problem with cooking a dish straight from frozen, especially a solid bake or pie, is that it can be more tricky to ensure it is heated right through. Liquid meals, such as soups or casseroles, can be defrosted over a gentle heat. You will need to watch them carefully in case they catch, and you may need to add extra liquid.

Vegetables should be cooked from frozen whenever possible, so they retain a fresher taste and crisper texture. Small savouries such as burgers can also be cooked from frozen.

Use your freezer for bulk cooking. For example, cook extra pulses and grains, then freeze those you don't need at the time. Bake double or triple batches of bread, cakes or pastries.

A freezer will also help you cope better if you have only one person who is vegetarian (or indeed one who eats meat!). You can make a variety of savouries and freeze them in suitable portions; this will save you preparing special meals every time.

MICROWAVE OVENS

Microwave ovens have changed from being a seemingly high-tech gadget to a useful, if not indispensable, piece of equipment in many kitchens. The microwave still suffers slightly from the fact that you can only make the most of it once you have experimented and understood it thoroughly, and that does take a while. I find I now use my microwave daily for all sorts of tasks to save time and washing up.

The microwave oven is marvellous for cooking vegetables as they remain crisp and bright. With a little practice, you can always serve them 'al dente'. Cooked in this way they retain a maximum amount of nutrients. I also use the microwave to soften vegetables to be stuffed, such as courgettes, peppers or cabbage leaves, as this saves blanching.

Many vegetarian recipes require sauces either as an integral part of the dish or as an accompaniment, and these are easy to make partly or completely in the microwave. It is very quick to make stock or to infuse milk to give sauces a better flavour. Roux-based sauces are easier to make as they are less likely to stick or burn.

I always toast nuts and seeds in the microwave and it is especially useful for making gomasio (see page 230). It saves time, too, when reconstituting dried fruit, either to plump up sultanas or raisins for a cake or sauce, or when you need a fruit purée as a sugar substitute.

Although it doesn't save any time when cooking pulses, whole grains or pasta initially, it is certainly quick to reheat them in the microwave, and their texture remains unspoilt. This means you can prepare more in advance if necessary and make the most of left overs. Processed cereals such as oatflakes or bulgar wheat can be easily and quickly cooked in the microwave too.

Baked or casseroled dishes can generally be microwaved. Remember that due to the speed of cooking, the flavours may not be fully developed. However, you can always make this sort of dish in advance and then reheat it.

Don't feel when tackling one recipe that you have to keep to either the microwave technique or to conventional methods of cooking on the hob or in the oven. Choose the best method for each stage of the recipe and you will end up saving time as well as making full use of your equipment.

Defrosting frozen food
Apart from being an invaluable cooking aid, one of the microwave's greatest assets is its speed in defrosting frozen foods – either single items or complete meals. It is worth choosing a microwave that has an automatic defrosting setting otherwise you will need to turn it on and off at short intervals. When freezing foods that are to be defrosted in the microwave, choose straight-sided shallow rather than deep dishes so the food gets maximum exposure to the microwaves. Round dishes are better than square ones, and don't use metal or foil containers. For easier defrosting of liquids, use a close fitting container so that the outsides cannot melt, spread out and then overcook or evaporate. When defrosting foods in a bag, pierce the bag to prevent it bursting.

Calculating defrosting times is a matter of experimenting. The greater the bulk of food, and the more dense it is, the longer it will take. It does help to stir, rearrange, separate out or turn the food over to ensure more even exposure to the rays.

EQUIPMENT

A batterie de cuisine is a very personal affair. I can never resist kitchen shops and always head straight for them, usually after visiting the local wholefood restaurant. I have picked up small items from around the world – wooden bowls and salad servers from Sweden, muffin tins from the United States, woks from Hong Kong.

It's no good collecting white elephants, but it is useful and time saving to have the right tools for the job. A good large knife and a solid chopping board are essential in the vegetarian kitchen, as are decent pans. I prefer stainless steel saucepans and a large non-stick frying pan, preferably with a lid. I also have a sturdy garlic press, a marble pestle and mortar, and plenty of wooden spoons. I like the type of peeler with a

floating blade, and often use a small paring knife and a serrated knife.

Many of these items do not demand a great outlay. However, electrical equipment is more expensive. There is now a vast range of gadgets to buy and I recommend having at least one of the following – a blender, food processor or food mixer and attachments. Do plan your kitchen so that these can be left ready to use or are easily accessible, so you can make the most of them. Of the other larger pieces of equipment, I have outlined their functions below and you may feel that some of them are worthwhile.

Blender or Liquidiser

An essential part of a vegetarian kitchen. Use it for making purées and smooth sauces, as well as for grinding nuts, breadcrumbs and cooked pulses. A blender saves an enormous amount of time and doesn't take up much space. Some blenders come with a coffee grinder; this is useful for grinding small quantities of nuts, seeds and spices.

Electric Steamer

Steaming is a long established method of cooking and an excellent way of retaining flavour and nutrients. Automatic steamers relieve you of the constant need to check the food and liquid level during cooking. They are also thermostatically controlled to ensure the correct temperature.

Food Mixer

As the name implies, a food mixer is useful for mixing batters, cake mixes and whisking eggs. The basic package includes a beater, whisk and a dough hook which is excellent for breadmaking, saving you time and energy. Extra attachments include a shredder and slicer, liquidiser goblet, juicer and grinder which makes the complete machine very versatile. You do need space for storing all the items with easy access or you may find them a nuisance to get out each time.

Food Processor

This is a versatile gadget having many functions including blending, grating and slicing. The food processor is also marvellous for rubbing in the fat in the initial stages of making pastry, taking just a few seconds. It is easy to process large quantities of nuts or bread, and very quick at grating cheese, carrots or slicing cabbage for coleslaw. If you are well organised and use the machine for dry ingredients before wet, you will save time on dismantling, cleaning and reassembly. I find the processor least satisfactory for blending such foods as nut milks and soups as it is difficult to obtain a completely smooth result.

Ice-Cream Maker

Although ice-cream makers are expensive pieces of equipment, they make marvellous ice-creams and sorbets, with superb textures. It is practically impossible to achieve this without the aid of a machine, especially in only 20 minutes. I am very fond of ice-cream and being concerned about the content of many commercial varieties I prefer to make my own so I am sure of the quality of the ingredients. Small hand-operated ice-cream makers are available which are effective and considerably cheaper than electric ones.

Juicer

Electric juicers are costly but certainly worth the expense if you enjoy really good fruit and vegetable juices. You also have the freedom to make all sorts of nutritious cocktails which are vastly superior to anything you can buy, unless it is freshly made in front of you.

Pasta Maker

Pasta can be made very successfully by hand, but rolling it out thinly takes practice and is hard work. A manual pasta machine makes this job very easy and a smooth even dough is obtained. Electric pasta makers are also available. These mix, cut and roll the pasta dough. However, they are expensive and probably not worth it for the occasional pasta meal.

Pressure Cooker

This is particularly useful for cooking beans and grains as it can cut the cooking time by about two-thirds. It is invaluable for making stocks and steamed puddings. Stainless steel varieties are also available.

Wok

A wok should not be seen as just a piece of equipment for oriental cookery, for it doubles up as a large frying pan and steamer. Woks are traditionally made from carbon steel, therefore they need to be looked after properly – seasoned initially and always wiped with a light coating of oil after use. Non-stick woks are now available which heat up quite quickly. The shape of the wok provides a large area for cooking and the sloping sides mean the food can be easily stirred round and cooked quickly with the minimum amount of oil or fat.

Yoghurt Maker

Although you can use a thermos flask, an electric yoghurt maker ensures the temperature is constant and more consistent results are achieved. The small pots are also useful for storing yoghurt in the refrigerator and for working out portions.

A–Z OF INGREDIENTS

Agar agar

A kind of gelatine derived from sea vegetables. Bought in flakes or powder form, it needs to be dissolved in boiling water before use otherwise it will not set. The setting powers are also affected by egg whites and acidic ingredients such as citrus juices. Two teaspoons agar agar should set 1 pint (570ml) liquid for jelly. There are other types of vegetable gelatines sold under brand names and available from health food shops.

Beansprouts

An excellent source of vitamins, minerals and valuable amounts of protein. Although mungbean sprouts are the best known, aduki beans, whole lentils, wheat grain, alfalfa and mustard and cress are other seeds that sprout well and taste quite different. To grow them at home, put seeds in a wide necked jar with a cloth to act as a strainer. Soak 1–2 tablespoons seeds overnight, then drain. Rinse the seeds 2 or 3 times daily in warm water, then drain them thoroughly; leaving the jar tipped permanently upside down is a good way to ensure this. If kept in a warm place, the seeds should sprout and be ready to eat in 4–7 days depending on the variety. Eat them, leaves and all. Any you don't want to use immediately can be stored in the refrigerator for up to 4 days. Use sprouts in salads, stir-frys or as crisp garnishes.

Carob

Carob pods are the dried seed pods of a tree principally found in the Mediterranean, Middle East and India. The pods turn brown in the autumn, are harvested and then cooked, roasted and ground to a fine powder. A darker powder with a stronger flavour comes from more highly roasted pods. Carob is used to give cakes, puddings and sauces a cocoa colour and as a substitute for chocolate flavour, although it is not really the same. The advantage of carob is that it is nutritionally superior to cocoa, containing no caffeine or theobromide which can trigger migraines. Carob flour will last several months. As it gets older it may become lumpy, in which case sieve the powder carefully.

Cheese

Vegetarian cheese, made with dairy milk but set with a vegetable rennet instead of an animal rennet, is becoming increasingly available. Some large supermarket chains sell vegetarian Cheddar, and wholefood and health food shops may stock vegetarian Cheshire, Double Gloucester,

Edam, Gouda and goat's cheese. The choice will probably depend on the supplier. Feta, the well known Greek cheese, is curdled without rennet as are several of the soft cheeses, namely curd cheese and ricotta. One organic cheese, made from an organically produced unpasteurised milk and with a similar flavour to Cheddar, is now nationally available.

Concentrated Apple Juice

This can be diluted to make drinks or used as a sweetener in cakes, puddings, sauces and dressings. Other concentrated fruit juices, such as pear or mixtures of apple and cherry or exotic fruits, are also available. When diluted they should be drunk within 24 hours. Keep the undiluted liquid in the refrigerator where, once opened, it should last 3–4 weeks.

Dried Fruit

A good source of natural sugar, vitamins, minerals and fibre. As these versatile foods keep up to a year, they are a useful part of any store cupboard. Use dried fruit straight from the packet for snacks, salads and baking. To reconstitute dried fruit, soak overnight in plenty of liquid or simmer for about 30 minutes in a covered pan. Serve as a fruit compote or purée for sauces and fillings. Some dried fruit sold is coated in mineral oils, so rinse well and sieve dry if necessary with flour. Wholefood and health food shops try to stock dried fruit that has undergone as little chemical treatment as possible.

Dried Mushrooms

These are important flavourings, often used in Japanese and Chinese cookery as well as the cuisines of central and southern Europe. There are many different types but they can be divided into two categories, wild and cultivated. They have a highly concentrated flavour and a robust texture. Soak dried mushrooms for at least 30 minutes before use, longer if possible. Add them to soups and casseroles along with the soaking liquid. Dried mushrooms can be bought in delicatessens, Chinese and Japanese grocers and some wholefood shops. They will keep up to one year and, although they are expensive, you don't need many.

Fromages Frais

These cheeses have become increasingly available in Britain, mainly in large supermarkets and delicatessens. Drained milk curds coagulated with lactic acids or rennet, they are uncooked and unripened. Some varieties have the consistency of yoghurt, others are much firmer. The fat content varies. Serve fromage frais alone for dessert or as a topping for fruit. You can also use it in dips, dressings and sauces, or as an ingredient in a savoury quiche or sweet cheesecake.

Gomasio

Sometimes known as sesame salt, gomasio is made by grinding roasted sesame seeds with salt. The ratio can be as little as one part salt to fourteen parts sesame seeds. It has a nutty flavour and is used as a seasoning or garnish for savoury dishes. An alternative is to roast the sesame seeds with a 2 inch (5cm) strip of kombu (a seaweed) and grind them together for a seaweed flavoured salt.

Grains

This group includes wheat, rice, barley, millet, rye, maize, oats and wild rice which are all from the family of grasses, and buckwheat which is the seed of a herbaceous plant. Unrefined grains are an important source of protein, fats, minerals and fibre. They can be bought whole, cracked, flaked or milled into meals and flours. Whole grains kept in cool, dry conditions will last indefinitely. Flakes and flours do not keep as well and are best used within 3–6 months. Grains are useful as accompaniments served plainly or with one or two additions, or as meals in themselves when cooked with vegetables, nuts or pulses. There are plenty of ideas for cooking grains on pages 84–99.

Margarine

Look out for margarines that are high in polyunsaturates and preferably choose ones with no colouring or flavourings added. These are generally available from health food and wholefood shops. Some soft margarines contain a high proportion of water and should not be used in baking.

Miso

A savoury paste derived from fermented soya beans, miso is one of the few plant sources of vitamin B12. Miso contains useful bacteria and enzymes that aid digestion. These are destroyed by boiling, so it is best to add miso at the end of cooking as a last minute seasoning. The paste is quite dense in texture, so dilute with water to make it easier to stir in. Add miso as a flavour enhancer for soups, casseroles and sauces. Serve it as a savoury spread but be aware that it is salty. Sold in jars or packets, miso will last for several months or even years if kept in the refrigerator.

Nuts and Seeds

Along with pulses and grains, these make an important contribution to a vegetarian diet as they are a good source of protein and fats. They may seem expensive but remember nuts and seeds are a concentrated food and only 1½–2oz (40–50g) is required per portion as the basis for a main meal. Each nut has an individual flavour and a slightly different nutritional profile but the main ones used in cooking – almonds, Brazils, cashews,

hazelnuts, walnuts, pecans and peanuts (strictly speaking a pulse) – are virtually interchangeable. However, chestnuts are quite unlike the others as they contain 50% water and are lower in fat and protein. Coconut is also different: it has a high fat content, which can be up to 98% saturated fat. Pine kernels have a very distinctive flavour and should be used sparingly, perhaps mixed with other nuts. Always buy nuts from a shop where the turnover is high as stale nuts go rancid quickly due to their high fat content. Whole nuts keep for up to 3 months; if flaked or ground, aim to eat them within 4–6 weeks.

Nut Butters

These are made from ground nuts with a little oil added. Peanut butter is the main one available but almond, cashew and hazelnut butters can be found. Nut butters from wholefood shops tend to be sugar free and often salt free, whereas supermarket versions may include up to 20% sugar. Use as sandwich spreads or flavourings for sauces and dressings.

Oils

Your choice of oil can greatly add to the nutrients in your diet as well as the flavour of your cooking. Varieties sold as cold pressed are high quality and have strong flavours. They are expensive and should be kept in a cool place. Refined or 'pure' oils are cheaper and have undergone chemical processes destroying certain nutrients and may well have pre-servative added to prevent them going rancid. In the middle price bracket are oils that are not cold pressed but do not contain anti-oxidents and anti-foaming agents. Safflower, soya and sunflower oil are all high in unsaturated fats, especially polyunsaturated. Rapeseed and olive oil have higher percentages of mono-unsaturated fats. Palm and coconut oil in particular should be avoided as they are high in saturated fats. Olive oil has a good flavour and is useful for salads and cooking. Safflower and sunflower oils are good all purpose oils with a delicate nutty flavour. Peanut oil is useful for frying as it can be heated to high temperatures without burning. Sesame oil is expensive, with a strong nutty flavour; a teaspoon or so can be used to flavour blander oils. Walnut and hazelnut oils, available in delicatessens and some herbalists, are full of flavour and quite delicious. Use them in salads.

Pasta

Pasta, the Italian word for dough, comes in an enormous variety of shapes. Dried varieties are readily available whereas there is still a limited selection of fresh wholewheat pasta. Dried pasta lasts for several months and makes a useful standby for emergency quick meals. There are plenty of ideas for using pasta on pages 72–82.

Pulses

Also known as legumes, pulses include beans, peas and lentils. They are an important source of protein for anyone eating little or no meat. Providing good quantities of unrefined carbohydrate, pulses are virtually fat free. Cooking instructions are included in specific recipes, but there are also some general rules. Always pick over the pulses for sticks and stones, then rinse thoroughly. Apart from lentils and split peas, all pulses should be soaked for at least 4 hours or overnight if possible. This gives them a chance to swell up properly and release certain indigestible starches into the soaking liquid. Throw away this liquid and rinse the pulses thoroughly. Bring them to the boil in plenty of fresh unsalted water. Boil fast for 10 minutes to destroy any toxins on the outer surface, then simmer until soft enough to bite through. The length of time will depend on the age and type of bean. Once cooked, drain well and use the cooking liquid as stock. The stock can be frozen or stored in the refrigerator for 3–4 days. Freeze cooked beans for up to 6 months or keep in the refrigerator for 3–4 days. A pound (450g) of dry beans will roughly double in weight once cooked.

Quark

This low-fat soft cheese, with a dry aftertaste and acidic tang, is made from skimmed milk. Quark is useful for making smooth cheese dressings as it blends more easily than cottage cheese.

Rennet

Used in most cheese-making as a coagulating agent. Animal rennet is obtained from the lining of a suckling calf's stomach. Vegetarian rennets are available and used in the making of vegetarian cheese.

Seaweed

More properly described as sea vegetables, seaweed contains valuable minerals. Dulse and wakame make good side vegetables, and you'll soon enjoy the flavour. Rinse and soak dried seaweeds briefly before using. Sold cleaned, dried and ready packaged, once opened they should be used within 4 months.

Shoyu and Tamari

These are naturally fermented soya sauces made from soya beans. Shoyu is usually mixed with wheat, whereas tamari is wheat free and has a stronger flavour. Both these products have strong salty tastes and can be used to enhance the flavour of many savoury recipes. Be careful with commercial soy sauces, which are often manufactured from synthetic ingredients and contain sugar, caramel and other additives.

Soya Milk

Low in fat, high in protein with a good vitamin and mineral content, soya milk is an easily digestible replacement for dairy milk. It can be made at home by soaking, boiling and straining ground soya beans, but commercial brands are increasingly available in wholefood shops, Chinese supermarkets and larger grocers. Soya milk is sold either plain or sweetened. Although the latter varieties are only very slightly sweetened, it is still best to use them in dessert recipes. Concentrated brands are also available which you can dilute yourself or use undiluted as a thick rich topping. Vegans, who do not use any animal products on moral grounds, use soya milk. It is also useful to the many people who suffer allergic reactions to cow's milk. Virtually any dairy recipe can be converted to use soya milk.

Stock Cubes and Vegetable Concentrates

These are used as a quick and convenient way to make stock and add flavour to soups and casseroles. The concentrates make a good savoury spread. Many supermarket brands contain monosodium glutamate and other taste enhancers so try to find additive-free varieties – they should be a concentration of vegetables, yeasts, vitamins and minerals only. Also available are stock powders which can be used in the same way as the cubes.

Sugar-Free Spreads and Low-Sugar Jams

Sugar-free spreads, sometimes sold as pure fruit spreads, have exactly the same function as jam. Their sweetness comes from a combination of a natural fruit flavour and concentrated fruit juices. Use as a healthy spread or sweetener in cakes and puddings. Sold in jars, once opened they should be kept in the refrigerator. They do not last for more than 3–4 weeks. Concentrated fruit spread, which has a consistency more like a yeast extract than a jam, will keep longer. Also available are jams with a lower proportion of sugar to fruit than usual, although they cannot be considered sugar free.

Tahini

A paste made from ground sesame seeds. It can be used on its own as a spread or mixed with other ingredients to make dips, sauces and pâtés. Available from health food and wholefood shops, there is both a pale and a dark variety; the colour depends on the treatment of the seed. The pale type has a milder, creamier flavour. Sometimes there will be a layer of oil on the top that has separated out; stir this in carefully before use. Tahini will keep for several months.

Tofu

A soya bean curd made from curdling warmed soya bean milk. The whey is strained off, leaving the soft curds. These are pressed under heavy weights until the texture is quite solid. Tofu is a valuable food containing protein, minerals such as potassium, magnesium and calcium, and the B vitamins. It is low in fat and contains no cholesterol. It is available in the refrigerated section of Chinese or Japanese stores or from wholefood or health food shops. Delicate in flavour, tofu's principle quality is that it will readily absorb other flavours. Tofu can be marinated, cooked in soups and casseroles, blended or mashed. Firm or regular tofu is hard enough to slice. Silken tofu, sold in long life tetra bricks, is more suitable for creams and dips. Once you have opened a packet of tofu, keep the remainder in a bowl of fresh water in the refrigerator. Change the water daily and it will last for up to 7 days. Tofu can be frozen but it becomes spongy and turns brown.

Yeast Extracts

These are made from brewer's yeast and are a good source of protein and minerals. They contain B vitamins and some brands have added B12 which is particularly useful for vegans. Generally yeast extracts have a high salt content but you can find varieties with less than 1% salt in wholefood and health food shops.

Yeast Flakes

Sold under the trademark Engevita, these tiny pale gold flakes have a delicious savoury flavour and will add a cheesy taste to white sauces, burger mixtures or quiche fillings. They can also be used as a garnish. The flakes are produced from a primary yeast grown from a mixture of molasses and cane and a solution of mineral salts. The yeast is then extracted by centrifugal force, washed to get rid of any molasses residue, then roller dried. Yeast flakes are sold in tubs or packets and, if kept cool and dry, they will last for up to 6 months.

Yoghurt

Made by fermenting milk with bacteria that produce lactic acid from the lactose the milk contains. The bacteria commonly used are Lactobacillus bulgarius and Streptococcus acidophilus. The milk used can be cow's, sheep's or goat's, and either full or low fat. Strained or hung yoghurt, originating in Greece and Cyprus, is ordinary yoghurt which has been strained to make it thicker and richer. Yoghurt can be easily produced at home using a bought culture, obtainable from health food shops, and warm milk and a thermos flask.

CONVERSION TABLES

All these are *approximate* conversions, which have either been rounded up or down. In a few recipes it may be necessary to modify them very slightly. *Never* mix metric and imperial measures in one recipe; stick to one system or the other.

Weights		Volume		Measurements	
½ oz	15g	1fl oz	25ml	¼ inch	0·5cm
1	25	2	50	½	1
1½	40	3	75	1	2·5
2	50	5 (¼ pint)	150	2	5
3	75	10 (½)	275	3	7·5
4	110	15 (¾)	400	4	10
5	150	1 pint	570	6	15
6	175	1¼	700	7	18
7	200	1½	900	8	20·5
8	225	1¾	1 litre	9	23
9	250	2	1·1	11	28
10	275	2¼	1·3	12	30·5
12	350	2½	1·4		
13	375	2¾	1·6	*Oven temperatures*	
14	400	3	1·75	Mark 1 275°F 140°C	
15	425	3¼	1·8	2 300 150	
1lb	450	3½	2	3 325 170	
1¼	550	3¾	2·1	4 350 180	
1½	700	4	2·3	5 375 190	
2	900	5	2·8	6 400 200	
3	1·4kg	6	3·4	7 425 220	
4	1·8	7	4·0	8 450 230	
5	2·3	8 (1 gal)	4·5	9 475 240	

INDEX

237